NEHRU AND THE CABINET MISSION

NEHRU AND THE CABINET MISSION

A ROAD TO INDIA'S FREEDOM STRUGGLE

SUBHAS CHANDRA MUKHOPADHYAY
M. A., Ph. 0.. D. Lilt.
Professor & Head, History Department
Vidyasagar University, Midnapur (W. Bengal)

GYAN

ISBN : 978-81-212-0387-6

Published, 2018

Published by

Gyan Publishing House
5, Ansari Road
Daryaganj, New Delhi-110002
Phone: 011-47034999, 9811692060
www.gyanbooks.com
E-mail: books@gyanbooks.com

Printed at: G. Print Process, Delhi.

To

THE MEMORY OF MY FATHER

BHOLA NATH MUKHERJEE

Born, Bagda, District Manbhum, Bengal, January 10, 1901

Died, Bagda, District Purulia, W. Bengal, January 31, 1983

who joined in the freedom struggle,

taught me to love the Indian people

and all peoples struggling for freedom

OTHER BOOKS OF THE AUTHOR

—*Career of Rajah Durlabhram Mahindra (Rai-Durlabh)*, Varanasi, 1974

—*Diwani in Bengal*, Varanasi, 1980

—*The Agrarian Policy of the British in Bengal, 1698-1772* Allahabad, 1987

—*British Residents at the Darbar of Bengal Nawabs at Murshidabad, 1757-1772*, Delhi, 1988

CONTENTS

PREFACE

The Cabinet Mission Plan was the first positive document for India's freedom, in which the Labour Prime Minister Attlee played a key role. In India, the political tangle for freedom became more acute for the opposite view of Nehru-Jinnah-Wavell, resulting the birth of a new state for the Muslims called Pakistan. Nehru—the idealist became disillusioned for the troubled situation, Jinnah, took to violence on the basis of his Two-Nation theory, while Wavell-the Viceroy as well as other leaders in Britain, differed fundamentally from the principles of the Cabinet Mission which they originally professed. It was no wonder that a truncated Pakistan had been born from the partition of India.

Jawaharlal Nehru played a key role in the struggle for India's freedom through negotiations with the British. His patriotism was beyond doubt. For over thirty years, he was India's foremost nationalist. He gave articulation and leadership to millions of people in India. He was the first statesman in the Afro-Asian world to lead his country along with an untrodden path of non-alignment. He was one of the leaders of humanism realising that imperialism was a curse and that nationalism should be poised on a sense of international community. He was the world's most committed enemy of imperialism. He was a man of intellect, honest and sincere.

The period 1945-47 was the most crucial for Nehru's life as well as the fate of India too. It was a period of India's march for freedom from foreign ycke. Thus the policy persuaded in 1945-47 had farreaching repurcussion on the history of free India. So under the present condition of our country's position, when we are at the end of the twentieth century, one has to reassess the events that took place on the eve of our independence. We committed some mistakes during our freedom struggle which can serve as an warning for future generations. The restless attitude of the present Indian provinces, particularly in the Punjab and Kashmir, is a clear indication of disruption of

Indian states. India won freedom through partition now posed as a great danger for our country. The Congress adopted the policy of negotiation with the British for which they could not make their will acknowledged rather the British dictated terms whatever they pleased. Jinnah was propagating his Two-Nation theory for the creation of Pakistan, though the League had not taken any part in the political struggle. Its' main object was to attack the Congress, which, according to them, was only national in name aiming at establishing Hindu Raj. On the other hand, Nehru was a great moralist. His speeches were sometimes less practical. He could not believe even when the Congress had decided for partition in March 1947 that a truncated Pakistan could ever be a reality. Thus Nehru and the Congress leaders were entraped under Jinnah's Two-Nation theory.

The history of Indian sub-continent has proved beyond doubt that the Two Nation theory of Jinnah has become a complete failure. Through this process, India gained her freedom but lost her unity. The creation of Pakistan, has weaken the position of the Muslims in India, There is still no indication that a strong and efficient government has been established in Pakistan. The creation of Pakistan has been the most unfortunate and unhappy development for the Muslims, which could neither solve the Hindu-Muslim enmity.

Some of the Congress leaders believed that the basis of partition was the enmity between the two communities as well as to end the civil wars in future. But the creation of Pakistan made this enmity permanent. Pakistan believes that for her existance, enmity with India is a necessity, for India may destroy her whenever she gets an opportunity. Similarly India also believes that whenever Pakistan gets an opportunity, she may move against India for attacking her.

Congress lacked firmness of decision and could not tackle the issues in time. They were not in a position to take force or resort to non-violence. On the other hand the League adopted violence and alarmed the British by the Great Calcutta-Killing in August 1946. Thus the vacilliating policy and at last the hasty decision (after Attlee's declaration) of the Congress, gave Jinnah the opportunity to enlist British support The leaders of the Congress, on the other hand, were divided among themselves, pulling in different directions by its left and right wings. The main problem was economic for both the communities which could bind them together, had been ignored. This proved very expensive for our freedom. Even Nehru had admitted in New York after India's independence in 1949 that he could not agree to India's partition, if he could foresee its evil consequences. (Pyarelal, *Mahatma Gandhi*, II, p. 156).

In preparing this monograph, I have taken help from various primary and secondary sources, all of them I have mentioned in the bibliography. I express my indebtedness to all those writers and institutions from whom I obtained valuable help. Some historians of note encouraged me immensely in preparing this work. Among them I am grateful to the retired Prof. B. K. Roy of L. N. Mithila University, Darbhanga, retired Prof. Hiralal Singh of Banaras Hindu University and retired Prof Zahiruddin Malik of Aligarh Muslim University. I also express my thanks to all my well wishers particularly to Prof. Suprakash Sanyal of Calcutta University and Prof. Chittabrata Palit of Jadavpur University. Prof. J. P. Mishra of Banaras Hindu University, sometimes encouraging, while often times criticising me for not undertaking an analytical approach on India's freedom movement.

Last but not the least I express my sincere gratitude to my wife Sandhya, and my daughter Sudipta, whose sincere help enabled me to complete this work with comparative ease. My father-in-law, Sri I. B. Banerjee, had taken much interest in the day to day progress of my work to whom I express my sincere gratitude. My two sons, Ashis and Soumen were also taken interest for the publication in this work. I am also grateful to Tara Printing Works, Varanasi, for Printing the book within shortest possible time.

S. C. Mukhopadhyay

Department of History
Vidyasagar University
Midnapore-721 101

Dol Purnima, February 28, 1991

ABBREVIATIONS

A. B. P.	Amrita Bazar Patrika.
ANM	Aggarwala, R. N., *National Movement and Constitutional Development of India.*
Azad, I. W. F.	Azad, Abul Kalam, *India wins freedom.*
Bandyopadhyay, *Jinnah*	Bandyopadhyay, Sailesh Kumar, *Jinnah : Pakistan, Natun Bhabna.*
Bright, *Important Speeches*	Bright, J. S., *Important Speeches of Jawaharlal Nehru.*
B. A. I.	Bright, J. S., *Before and after Independence.*
De, *Aami Subhas*	De, Sailesh, *Aami Subhas Bolchhi.*
Dorothy, *Nehru*	Norman, Dorothy, *Nehru—the first sixty years.*
Ghosh, I. N. A.	Ghosh, K. K., *The Indian National Army.*
GIC	Gwyer Maurice and A. Appadorai, *Speeches and Documents on the Indian Constitution.*
I. A. R.	*Indian Annual Register.*
Kamaruddin, *East Pakistan*	Ahmad Kamaruddin, *The Social history of East Pakistan.*
Lumby, *Transfer of Power*	Lumby, E. W. R., *The Transfer of power in India.*
MTP	Menon, V. P., *The Transfer of power in India.*
MBN	Brecher, Michael, *Nehru, a political biography.*
Moon, *Gandhi*	Moon, Penderel, *Gandhi and Modern India.*
MJN	Moraes, Frank, *Jawaharlal Nehru.*

Mosley, *The British Raj*	Mosley, Leonard, *The last days of the British Raj.*
Muller, I. W. I.	Muller, Eward and Bhattacharjee, Arun, *India wins Independence.*
NMG	Nanda, B. R., *Mahatma Gandhi-a Biography.*
Pandey, *Nehru*	Pandey, B. N. *Nehru.*
Pyarelal, Mahatma Gandhi	Pyarelal, *Mahatma Gandhi-the last phase.*
S. W. J. N.	S. Gopal, *Selected works of Jawaharlal Nehru*
S. I. N. C.	Sitaramayya, Pattabhi, *History of Indian National Congress.*
Toye, S. T.	Toye, Hugh, *The Springing Tiger.*
V. I.	*Voice of India.*
W. V. J.	Wavell, Lord, *The Viceroy's Journal.*
Woolpert	Woolpert, Stenley, *Jinnah of Pakistan.*

CHAPTER I

1945-46 : YEARS OF MOUNTING TENSIONS

Jawaharlal Nehru came out from prison from Almorah District jail[1] with other Congress leaders on June 15, 1945, and faced a different political situation prevalent during the time of the Quit India Movement of 1942. During this period many eventful incidents of note passed within the country, making the situation more complex. The Congress organisation was banned during the war and except Gandhiji, almost all Congress leaders were in jail. The Muslim League, was campaigning for Pakistan, but its target was the Congress. In six provinces constitutional government was in abeyance ; while in the remaining five, ministers friendly to the British government were in power. The appointment of Lord Wavell as the Viceroy of India in October 1943, disgusted Nehru ; because the new Viceroy had no sympathy for India and her leaders. He was the commander-in-chief of British India since January 1941 and saw the country through a soldier's eyes. He found in Gandhi nothing but hypocrisy, Jinnah was proud and vain, Nehru was honest but too much of an idealist. Wavell understood, in his own way that there was no chance of solution of Indian problems, till the three were out of the way.[2]

The Congress ideals of "Do or die" during the Quit India Movement, failed to achieve any result. The Congress hoped that this movement might create an impact on the Muslims, also proved empty, as because the Muslim League did not participate in this movement. The Muslims were told that it was a shameful attempt of the Congress to capture power

1. It was Madam Chiang Kai Shek who agitated for Nehru's release. Nehru had a cordial relation with General Chiang Kai-Shek, the latter pressed the British government for India's independence.
2. Wavell, Lord, *The Viceroy's Journal*, Edt. by Penderal Moon London, 197-), p. 79.

from the British and establish a Hindu Raj.[3] The British rulers, on the other hand, tried to protect the interests of the Muslim League because of their dissociation from the Congress movement. It meant that the British administrators though professed for the unity of India, would not transfer power to Congress alone if such circumstance would occur in the arena of Indian politics.

Muslim League, after the failure of the Quit India Movement of the Congress and the end of World War II, vigorously persuaded the creation of a separate state for them, in the form of Pakistan, where they could live against the tyranny of the Hindus. To Jawaharlal, this movement of the Muslims seemed disastrous as he believed that the sentiment of regionalism had been created artificially, which had no permanent bearing on the Muslims. On the other hand, he believed in world organisations where Pakistan had no place in the logic of world progress. Nehru visualised India playing a great role in world organisations. Though Indians did not show the same sort of vigour like the Americans, Russians or the Chinese, he believed that the inherent spirit of the Indians needed only to be re-charged, and "waken her from her long slumber."[4]

The Simla Conference held in June-July 1945, soon failed due to Jinnah's persistant claim of parity between the caste Hindus and the Muslims Neither Wavell, nor the Congress agreed to accept this principle and as a result, the Congress felt that the Pakistan issue had been put in a cold storage for ever. But within a short time they realised their mistake. It took Nehru some time to realise that the voluntary exile of the Congress from politics had strengthened Jinnah's Pakistan movement.

3. *Ibid.*, pp 32–34.
4. Nehru, Jawaharlal, *Discovery of India* (Reprint, Bombay, 1967), p. 58. Like Nehru, Gandhiji had also no faith in Pakistan. When asked about the Two-nation theory of Jinnah, Gandhiji reacted sharply by remarking that a change of religion did not change nationality.

After the surrender of Germany in May, Britain had decided to go to polls. The election took place under the caretaker government of Churchill. In the election campaign, the Labour Party stressed the need of resolving the Indian problem as soon as Japan would surrender. The voting took place on July 5 and tho Labour Party emerged victorious, capturing 393 seats as against 213 by the conservatives. On July 26, Clement Attlee was announced as the Prime Minister of Britain. The King's speech on the opening of the new Parliament was momentus : "In accordance with the promises already made to my Indian people, my Government will do their utmost to promote in conjunction with the leaders of Indian opinion, early reallzation of full self government in India."[5]

Atom bomb forced Japan to surrender and the war came to a close.[6] Soon after, the Labour Government announced its verdict for "an early realisation of self-government in India."[7] As a proof of their good gesture, the British government summoned Wavell to England and before his return to India, a fresh election was announced in India both to the Central and the Provincial legislatures. Wavell soon after his return to India, gave his broadcast speech on September 19, on the following purport : "It is the intention of His Majesty's Government to convene as soon as possible a Constitution Making Body, and as a preliminary step they have authorised me to undertake immediately after the elections, discussions with the representatives of the Legislative Assemblies in the Provinces."[8]

5. Sitaramayya, Pattabhi, *History of the Indian National Congress*, Vol. II (New Delhi, 1969), p. 667.
6. When Gandhiji was asked about the Atom bomb, he said that he was not disturbed by it. On the contrary he felt more certain than ever that after that nothing else was left for mankind but to adopt non-violence.
7. Moon, Penderel, *Gandhi and Modern India* (London, 1968), p. 240.
8. S.I.N.C., Vol. II, p. 667.

The Prime Minister, Attlee, at the same time announced on September 19 that the British government had given an immediate attention in the Constitution-Making body of India as was the declared policy of the government :

"The first step necessary", he announced, "is to get as soon as may be as democratic a representation of the Indian peoples as possible...... Therefore, it has already been announced, elections will be held in India in the coming cold weather." He announced further about the noble intention of the British Government, adding that "the Government has authorised Lord Wavell to undertake preliminary discussions with representatives of new Provincial Legislatures, as soon as they are elected to ascertain whether the proposals of the Cripps' offer are acceptable as they stand, or whether some alternative or modified scheme should be preferable." In the same speech Attlee further added that "the Government has further authorised the Viceroy as an interim measure to take steps after the elections to bring into being an Executive Council, having the support of the main Indian parties, in order that India may deal herself with her own social and economic problems and may take her full part in the working out a New World Order."[9]

These announcements affirmed the determination of the British government to grant self-government to India after the general election. Thus the British government gave assurances to the Indians of two vital importance, namely, a Constituent Assembly was to be set up to frame the constitution of an independent India ; while the other was to form a provisional government with the support of the main Indian parties. Thus the parties concerned became juvilent on the future outcome of the Indian election. The Congress was not in a mood to launch a new movement, but to participate in the general election. A majority of the Congress leaders including Nehru and Gandhiji believed to devote themselves in constructive work. "They believed that there was not much hope on the

9. *Ibid.*, pp. 669–670.

political plane."[10] Nehru made his own plan and calculated that if the Congress could win all the general seats in the Provincial and Central legislatures with a considerable number of Muslim seats, then the Muslim League as the sole representative of the Muslim community would not stand. Jinnah would not force his bargaining power if he failed to capture the majority of Muslim seats. But at the same time, if Jinnah could gain majority in the Punjab election, Nehru would assure Jinnah about the Muslims parity with the Hindus, other rhan scheduled casts, in the government.[11]

With this end in view Nehru tried to popularise Congress among the masses. He left the politics of management to Ballabhbhai Patel and Rajendra Prasad, but never permitted them to compromise at the cost of the ideals of the Congress. He wanted to project among the Muslims the secular image of the Congress. And as a proof of it, he ruled out the proposal of Rajendra Prasad that Congress should make pact with Hindu Mahasabha. In this way, Nehru thought that the Congress must disprove the allegation that it was a Hindu organisation[12] But when all these election procedures had been taking shape within the Congress, the general mass of India became alarmed to learn that the victims of the Indian National Army had been accused and brought to Delhi for trial on the ground of waging war against the Allied Powers.

The arrest and subsequent trials of the I. N. A. soldiers in the Red Fort at Delhi, created great furore within the length and breadth of the country. In fact there was not a soul in India who was not stirred by the vigour and spirit of the army. Day in and day out, the people began to listen the radios for the development of the trials. The people of India began to argue

10. Azad, Abul Kalam, *India Wins Freedom* (New Delhi, Reprinted 1989), p. 128. (The present edition includes 30 pages of Azad's statement that had been released after thirty years of his death.)
11. W. V. J., p. 199.
12. Nehru's letter to Rajendra Prasad, Oct. 9, 1945 (Prasad Papers).

about the rights of a subject nation to wage war for its freedom. There was widespread agitation for the suspension of the trials as well as for their liberations. These agitations led to nationwide demonstration in favour of the release of the I.N.A. soldiers, resulting in the shooting in Calcutta where forty people died and over three hundred were injured. Soon the news of Calcutta killing reached in Bombay, where twenty-three persons were killed while many injured.[13]

The history of the I.N.A. and its leader, Subhas Chandra Bose had its own charm that made the Indian people spell bound during its trials. During a whole year of Presidentship of the Indian National Congress, from Haripura to Tripuri, Subhas found himself out of tune with Gandhian line, His thought of freedom was different from Gandhi. With Gandhi 'means are ends', while with Subhas 'ends are means'. This difference of the two polar opposites has been summed up by Sitaramayya : "Gandhi is moved by instinct, Subhas was guided by reason. He (Subhas) felt that there was a deplorable lack of clarity in the plan which the Mahatma had formulated and that he himself did not have a clear idea of the successive stages of the campaign which would bring India to her cherished goal of Freedom. That was not merely Subhas's complaint. It is a general complaint against Gandhi. Indeed whenever Gandhi was asked in 1922 about Mass Civil Disobedience, he said he himself did not know. His is rather the trend of a motor driver driving his car in a fog where he is able to see only 10 yards ahead and then another ten and then another ten until he reaches his goal."[14]

13. S.I.N.C., II, P. 678. The riot in Calcutta had been broken due to the indiscriminate shooting in the military camp of Nilganj near Calcutta, where nearly one thousand of I.N.A. soldiers were kept in arrest. On September 25, five I.N.A. soldiers were assassinated. This led to widespread discontent and even the loyal Gorkha regiment stationed at Dehradun also joined with the civilian population against the British Government. De, Sailesh, *Aami Subhas Bolchi* (In Bengali, Calcutta 3rd Edn. 1389 B. S.) P. 407.

14. *Ibid.*, pp. 678-679.

But Subhas was a different sort of man, every inch a man that did not shine by reflected light.

Subhas was a born leader. When he assumed the post of the commander-in-chief of the I. N. A.[15], the army had no high morale, or discipline. But within a short time, he infused a new spirit in them so that it became a real revolutionary force. Its strength increased and its morale rose as it became the army of a Provisional Government. "The leader gave the army a sense of pride, a battle-cry and helped it realise for the first time the significance of its revolutionary role."[16] It was thus no wonder that when the Subhas's army was brought for trials they did not repent for their action. The Indian people with full sympathy towards them, did not tolerate such humiliation of the freedom fighters. Even the Indian services gradually "came to have a certain sympathy with the popular clamour about the I.N.A., which was being raised in India."[17] Even Gandhiji's whole outlook on Subhas had undergone a change who admired the resourcefulness of Subhas.[18]

On November 5, 1945, three leading I. N. A. victims, Col. Shah Nawaz, Captain Seghal and Lt. Dhillon were brought to Delhi for trials. Besides another batch of I. N. A. officials like Major-General Kiwani, Major-General Chatterjee, General Bhonsle, Abid Hasan, Pritam Singh, Guljara Singh and Deb-nath Das, ware arrested from different places of South-east Asia, also brought to Delhi for trials.

But in India, the I. N. A. had become a symbol of unity among the various religious groups who represented Hindus,

15. Subhas became the Commander-in-Chief of the I. N. A. on August 25, 1943.
16. Ghosh, K. K. *The Indian National Army*, p. 2:0.
17. Toye, Hugh, *The Springing Tiger* (Bombay, 1959), p. 170.
18. About Gandhiji's view on Subhas, Azad remarks : "I saw that Subhas Bose's escape to Germany had made a great impression on Gandhiji. He had not formerly approved many of his remarks convinced me that he admired the courage and resourcefulness of Subhas. His admiration of Subhas Bose unconsciously coloured his view."—Azad, I. W. F., p. 40.

Muslims, Sikhs and Christians. The victims of the I. N. A. who were brought to Delhi soon overshadowed the names of national leaders. It looked as though the I. N. A. itself eclipsed the Indian National Congress and the exploits of war and violence abroad threw into obscurity the victories of non-violence at home."[19]

Originally Nehru had neither any sympathy nor faith with the I. N. A. He proclaimed that the I. N. A. had chosen a wrong path in fighting against the Allied powers and a number of soldiers including its leaders were misguided by joining hands with Japan. He described their activities as most unfortunate. But within a short time, this view of Nehru underwent a little change. "In a wave of nationalist emotion, the I. N. A. were acclaimed heroes who had fought for the freedom of India, no political leader who valued his future could stand aloof—all must offer to defend the martyrs."[20] The leaders of the Congress began to collect subscriptions for I. N. A. Defence Fund and accordingly I. N. A. Flag Days were celebrated.

An I. N. A. Defence Committee consisting of Bhulabhai Desai[21], Kailashnath Katju, Tej Bahadur Sapru, Raghunandan Saran, Asaf Ali and Jawaharlal Nehru was formed. They declared that the object of the I. N. A. was the same as that of the Congress, the independence of the country and as such they had sided with the victims of the I. N. A. Thus Nehru also emotionally had been drawn towards them believing that on the eve of a general election, a political party was sure to win popular support in defending the I. N. A. When the

19. S. I. N. C., Vol. II, p. 784.
20. Toye, S. T., p. 182.
21. The services rendered by Bhulabhai Desai were of inestimable value, who made the Indian people acquainted about the daily developments of I. N. A. trials. Presenting the defence argument on December 17 and 18, before the General Court Martial, Desai argued that the I. N. A. members fought for the liberation of their country. He claimed that the officers might be treated as prisoners of war and set free with the cessation of hostilities.

actual trials of the I. N. A. began, Nehru donned his barrister's gown and appeared as one of the defence counsels. The British government did not dare to convict the I. N. A. officials and on January 4, 1946, only three leaders were acquitted.[22]

Due to political reasons Nehru joined the I. N. A. trials to support their cause, and it seemed that his attitude towards them had been liberal at that time. But Nehru had no fixed attitude towards the Indian National Army. In March 1946, Nehru went out of his visit to Malaya, where he met Lord Mountbatten. Nehru wanted to unveil a memorial to the Indian National Army that embarrassed Mountbatten[23], the latter forbade him from laying a wreath on the I. N. A. memorial, advising him : "The I. N. A. were not politically conscious heroes fighting for their country but cowards and traitors who betrayed their loyal friends." Nehru agreed to this point, when Mountbatten further advised him ; "The people who will serve you well in your national army of the future are those who are loyal to their oath ; otherwise if you become unpopular a disloyal army may turn against you."[24] Nehru also realised the validity of this advice[25] and accordingly he did not allow the Indian National Army men to rejoin the army of an independent India. But Nehru did not make any bar of I. N. A. personnel to join in other civil employments, as his subsequent letter, as the head of the Interim-Government, written to Ballabhbhai Patel, would testify : "I understand that subsequently it was made clear to Provincial Governments that there should be no bar at all to the employment of I. N. A. personnel, except in so far as the army or the police services were concerned. Some of the Provincial Governments have

22. De, *Aami Subhas*, p. 427.
23. Norman, Dorothy (Edt.), *Nehru : The First Sixty Years*, Vol. II (Bombay, 1965), p. 219.
24. Hodson, H. V., *The Great Divide : Britain-India-Pakistan* (London, 1969), p. 205.
25 Nehru could not openly defy the advice of Mountbatten, but privately visited the I. N. A. memorial and placed some flowers there.

actually employed them in various civil departments."[26] Replying to Nehru's letter, Ballabhbhai informed him, "So far as the Home Department was concerned there was no ban on the re-employment of ex-I. N. A. personnel,"[27]

Still there were a number of I. N. A. officials, who remained in prisons. Nehru wanted to release all of them, though he had a sharp difference of opinion with the British commander-in-chief, the latter wanted to examine the merits of each detenu. Writing to Baldev Singh, Nehru emphasised the need of their release: "Both the Congress members and the Muslim League members, as well as others, would, normally speaking, have unanimously passed the resolution asking for their release." In the same letter, Nehru expressed his anxiety: "It is exceedingly difficult for us to ignore a very widespread public sentiment. The result of ignoring it is bound to lead public agitation and possibly some trouble."[28] Some of the Congress leaders argued that the British government could not complain against the conduct of the I.N.A. officers. They had been sent to Burma and Singapore by the order of the British government. When Japan occupied these regions, the British government left these soldiers to their fate. So if they had sided with the Japanese under duress, such action seemed justified. They organised a separate Liberation Army of India. It meant that if the British were driven out of India, the country would not be occupied by the Japanese but by an Indian National Army.[29]

According to the list prepared by the I.N.A. Headquarters, there were 35,000 I. N. A. officials still in detention all over India. The Central Legislative Assembly as early as on February 4, 1946, moved a resolution, headed by Govind Malviya, recommending that the Government should give up the trials

26. Nehru's letter to Ballabhbhai Patel, November 15, 1946 (vide, S. Gopal (Edt), Selected Works of Jawaharlal Nehru, Vol. I, p. 355.
27. S. W J. N., Vol. I, p. 355).
28. Nehru's letter to Baldev Singh, December 25, 1946.
29. Azad, I. W .F., p. 143.

of the officers of the Indian National Army and release them immediately. But Wavell held the view that any concession to the I. N. A. men or their release from prison would make it impossible for the commander-in-chief to remain responsible for the discipline of the Indian army.[30] The situation continued in such a way for full one year, and when Nehru became practically the head of the Interim government, made a draft note for the Cabinet wherein he suggested : "In view of this situation, the inevitable conclusion arrived at are that the I. N. A. prisoners serving their sentences at present should be released.'[31]

During the winter months of 1945-46, tensions in the country had been steadily gaining momentum. In the beginning of 1946 there was a mounting wave of student demonstration, strikes and violence, combined with the revolt of the Indian Navy. The sailors of Bombay were influenced by the trial and conviction of Bose's Indian National Army officers, unfurled the standard of rebellion.[32] The position of the Congress leaders became more difficult, while the I. N. A. activities caused manifold difficulties for the British-even the Viceroy became convinced that India could no longer be held by the Indian military and naval forces. It was the Royal Air Force in Calcutta, who in early 1946, mutined in the city. Such disruptive action soon spread elsewhere in India followed by the hungor strikes in the Royal Indian Air Force. It was soon followed by a naval mutiny in Bombay, the incident occurred on February 18, which had a far reaching consequence. Within five days from this incident, both the leading base of the Royal Indian Navy of Bombay. "presented the appearance of a minor battlefield."[33]

There were genuine grievances at the root of the mutiny, among them two were of such importance that went against the British imperialism. They demanded acquittal of all I.N.A.

30. S. W. J. N., vol. I, p. 357.
31. Nehru's Draft note for Cabinet (S. W. J. N., vol. 1,p. 371).
32. "There can be little doubt that the serious naval mutinies and the unrest in other two services early in 1946, owed something to its I.N.A. influence"—Toye, S. T., p. 170.
33. Dorothy, *Nehru*, Vol. 11, p. 201.

officers with immediate effect, while the other was to recall the Indian soldiers that had been sent to Indo-China for the help of the French government there.[34] Within a short time, the mutiny involved the whole navy.[35] The situation of the naval mutiny became more critical, when the left-wing parties called for a "union of Hindus and Muslims at the barricades." Communists began to support the Sailors' Central Strike Committee, while the Congress leaders sympathized with the sailors grievances, but did not like their link with the Communists.

Nehru had sympathy with the sailors, but at the same time he believed that some anti-social elements had exploited the situation, making the condition worse for India's fight for freedom. "The time has come," he exclaimed, "when we should direct our energies along the channel of constructive work. What happened in Bombay shows that the constructive tendency is lacking." He gave foremost importance to India's freedom, the other petty problems would solve in a peaceful way. "For the past twenty-five years," Nehru went on explaining his own view, "the people of India have made tremendous sacrifices in the cause of winning our national independence. Our freedom is near at hand to-day. We have all the virtues for winning our freedom, but I confess that we lack the discipline which is essential for a free country."[36]

When asked in a Press Conference on March 1, 1946, Nehru expressed his serious concern on 'naval ratings' and began to apprehend victimisation from the British government. Attempts had already been made by the government to terrorise the mutiners as well to inflict punishment on them. It was also suggested by the government even "of punishing people

34. De, *Aami Subhas*, p. 435.
35. "The Mutiny in fact, involved the whole navy. Seventy-eight ships of various description stationed in Bombay, Karachi, Madras, Calcutta, Cochin, Vizagapatam, Andamans and almost all naval shore establishments in the country joined the mutiny."—Ghosh, I.N.A., P. 232.
36. Moraes, Frank, *Jawaharlal Nehru* (New York, 1956), p. 314.

against whom there is no evidence," with the object of frightening and terrorising others. But if the British government would adopt such a course, Nehru believed that the action would obviously be "in direct conflict both in spirit and letter with the assurances given in the Assembly."[37] But in such cases of victimisation and trial, Nehru advocated a Defence Committee for the accused.

At this time, Nehru began to preach among the people the theory of non-violence. He believed that there was a clear-cut difference between violence and non-violence, which some people could not understand. In India's fight for freedom, non-violence was the only desirable technique, both in regard to the internal conditions in India and in regard to world affairs. "It seems to me obvious that if one thinks in terms of violence, one must think in terms of superior violence." Nehru made his point clear by adding further · "It is folly to put up inferior violence to oppose superior violence."[38] And in moment of crisis one might think not in terms of a particular crisis, but in terms of a general policy. At the present juncture of India's politics, Nehru believed that the non-violence was the only policy which the people of India might adopt[39] for the freedom of their country.

Patel had great dislike to the socialists on idcological ground. He severely criticised some of them, particularly to Mrs. Aruna Asaf Ali and her group, who, according to him, were gaining cheap popularity by making wild speeches. Patel held them responsible for inciting the ratings of the navy in Bombay and some other places to revolt. When troops were called to suppress the revolt, the mutineers openly defied them. During this time Patel intervened and asked the mutineers to laid down their arms. Patel feared a revolution in the country with which the whole atmosphere was then surcharged and to avoid chaos, he wanted the socialists to be restrained in time.

37. Dorothy, *Nehru* II, p. 202.
38. Quoted in *Ibid.*, p. 205.
39. Amrita Bazar Patrika (Calcutta), March 1, 1946.

But Nehru did not like this idea of Patel, however misguided the socialists were, as some of them including Mrs. Aruna Asaf Ali were his friends.[40]

The Congress once more tried to combat these disorders and the doctrine of non-violence was preached upon. In a resolution drafted by Gandhiji, the working committee of the Congress explained that "non-violence does not include burning public property, cutting of Telegraph wires, derailing trains and intimidation." Emphasis was laid on constructive programme and the removal of untouchability. When Gandhiji reproached the mutineers with "setting a bad and unbecoming example," Patel personally intervened to quell the naval mutiny and to prevent strikes. Gandhiji warned the country: "The rulers have declared their intention to Quit. Let not the action be delayed by a moment because of the exhibition of this distressful unrest."[41]

On the question of general election in India, Congress became busy in preparing the election campaign during the winter of 1945-46 but it became somewhat delayed due to the increasing tensions in I. N. A. trials. The Congress Working Committee had published a manifesto for the Central Elections and soon afterwards, published a composite manifesto on December 22, 1945, covering the central as well as provincial elections. The manifesto declared the achievements of the Congress during last sixty years: "For sixty years the National Congress has laboured for the freedom of India. During this long span of years its history has been the history of the Indian people... From small beginnings it has progressively grown and spread in this vast country, carrying the massage of freedom to the masses of our people .. By service and sacrifice it has enshrined itself in the hearts of our people." The manifesto promised "equal rights and opportunities for every citizen of India, man and woman." It also assured constitutional rights

40. Letter from Mrs. Aruna Asaf Ali to Nehru, December 8, 1945 (Nehru Papers).
41. Moon, *Gandhi*, p. 241.

providing fundamental rights of every citizen of India. The manifesto further pointed out numerous problems during "a hundred and fifty years and more of foreign rule" that arrested the progress of the country. A vast country like India had not only been politically dominated and humiliated, but it had also suffered "economic, social, cultural and spiritual degradation." The Congress wanted to solve these problems : "Industry and agriculture, the social services and public utilities must be encouraged, modernised and rapidly extended in order to add to the wealth of the country and give it the capacity for self-growth, without dependence on others. But all this must be done with the primary object of benefitting the masses of our people and raising their economic, cultural and spiritual level, removing unemployment, and adding to the dignity of the individual. For this purpose it will be necessary to plan and co-ordinate social advances in all its many fields, to prevent the concentration of wealth and power in the hands of individuals and groups, to prevent vested inimical to society from growing, and to have social control of the mineral resources, means of transport and the principal methods of production and distribution in land, industry and in other departments of national activity, so that free India may develop into a co-operative commonwealth." After issuing this manifesto, the Congress appealed to the people to support the Congress candidates at the forthcoming general elections : "The Congress, therefore, appeals to the voters all over the country to support Congress candidates in every way at the forthcoming elections, and to stand by the Congress at this critical juncture which is so pregnant with future possibilities.[42]

The election results, however, did not give full satisfaction to Nehru, it neither gave overwhelming joy to Jinnah as there was no clear verdict in favour of Pakistan. In the Central Assembly the Congress won fifty-seven general seats, but failed to secure any Muslim seat, all thirty were won by the

42. The Congress Manifesto, December 11, 1945, Quoted from Sitaramayya, I. N. C., Vol. II, Appendix I, pp. i-v; also in Azad, I. W. F., pp. 130-32.

Muslim League. Jinnah was also to some extent disappointed, for what matters to the League in terms of Pakistan was not secured in the Central but in the provincial legislatures, particularly those provinces which Jinnah claimed for Pakistan. In the provinces, the League captured 446 Muslim seats out of 495.[43] In Punjab the League secured 79 out ot 86 Muslim seats. In the Punjab where the Unionists remained in power for a number of years, the League came out as the largest single party, falsifying the claim of the Unionists to speak for the Muslims of the Punjab. But the League failed in the North-Western Frontier Province, where the influence of the Khan brothers and *Khudai Khidmatgars* was still supreme. In the North-Western Frontier Province the League secured 17 out of 38, in Sind 28 out of 34, in Bengal 113 out of 119. In Assam, which Jinnah claimed for Pakistan, the League secured 31 out of 34 Muslim seats; but Congress retained an over-all majority by winning 58 seats. The Congress retained a mejority of seats in all the other provinces except in Punjab where a coalition government was formed under Khizar Hyat Khan Tiwana.[44]

In the general elections, Muslim parties other than the League were virtually eliminated and Jinnah's claim that he was the sole representative of the Muslims in India was firmly es ablished. Now the crucial question was whether India should remain united or be divided. Jinnah claimed that the League "could settle the Indian problem in ten minutes", if Gandhi would agree for Pakistan. If Gandhi would say, "I agree that one-fourth of India, composed of six provinces Sind, Baluchistan, the Punjab, the North-Western Frontier Province, Bengal and Assam— with their present boundaries constitute the Pakistan state." But Gandhi did say nothing of this kind, he was still in the hope of a united India, while

43. Moon, *Gandhi*, p. 240.
44. Pandey, B. N., *Nehru* (London, Reprint, 1977), p. 256. Also, Aggarwala, R. N., *National Movement and Constitutional Development of India* (Delhi, 2nd Edn. 1955, pp. 244-245.

Patel thought that Jinnah was still bluffing, who might "accept something less than Pakistan".[45]

While the mounting tensions in India was gradually increasing, the British government gave a further indication of its desire to solve the problem of Indian independence. On February 19, 1946, it was announced in both houses of British Parliament that "in view of the paramount importance not only to India and to the British Commonwealth but to the peace of the world of a successful outcome of the discussions with the leaders of the Indian opinion," the Government had decided to send a special mission of Cabinet Ministers "to seek an association with the Viceroy an agreement with these Leaders on the principle and procedure relating to the Constitutional issue". The name of the members of the Mission consisting of Lord Pethick-Lawrence-the Secretary of State for India, Sir Stafford Cripps - the President of the Board of Trade and Mr. A. V. Alexander - the First Lord of the Admiralty were announced.[46]

Further statements by the British added some new light upon the nature of the Mission's task, which was to help the Viceroy in giving effect to the programme outlined in his statement of September 19, 1945 that was for bringing a Constitution-making body and secondly, an interim Executive Council supported by the main Indian parties : Preparatory discussions with elected representatives of British India and with Indian States in order to secure the widest measure of agreement as to the method of framing a Constitution," and secondly, "the setting up of a Constitution-making body and third, the bringing into being of an Executive Council having the support or the main Indian parties."[47] There was however one point in the previous Cripps offer, which was reaffirmed more unambiguously that "India would be at liberty to choose

45. Moon, *Gandhi*, p. 240.
46. Dorothy, *Nehru*, Vol. II, p. 205.
47. S. I. N. C., Vol. II, Appendix-IV, p. cxlvi.

her own future position in the world, whether inside or outside the Commonwealth."[48]

But inspite of the announcement of the Cabinet Mission, anti-British demonstrations continued in India throughout the remainder of February.

---

48. Lumby, E. W. R., *The Transfer of Power in India* (London, 1954), pp. 71–72.

CHAPTER II

THE CABINET MISSION PLAN

When the news of the announcement of the formation of the Cabinet Mission in England reached India, Nehru became very much hopeful and believed that a satisfactory solution of the Indian problem would be evolved[1] by the efforts of the Mission with the Indian leaders. But at the same time, on the question of the prospect of success of the proposed Mission, Nehru warned his countrymen that the British Delegation might work "for the interest of Britain" only and so the Indian delegates must meet them for the interests of India. Britain claimed an undue superiority and might try to impose her own will." In a Press Conference, Nehru advised the people to be cautious about this attitude: "Britishers even today...... cannot get rid of their tradition which has eaten into their minds and they still talk of India often enough in a language (reminiscent) of a generation or two ago. They forget that they are addressing a sensitive, proud and virile people who will not put up with any patronage or anything smacking of superiority."[2] Nehru also firmly believed that India would be free "in the course of next years", but it was finally dependent on British attitude towards India. If Britain was to adopt an hostile attitude, India might go against her, but if on the other hand, she became friendly to India, the latter might follow a policy of co-operation. "If India gains her independence inspite of Britain, India for a long time is likely to be a country hostile to Britain, ranged in a camp hostile to Britain in the world context. On the other hand, if India attains independence more or less immediately by cooperating with the British, it might be possible for Britain to salvage some goodwill,

1. Press Conference of Nehru, February 27, 1946.
2. Quoted in Dorothy, *Nehru*, II, p. 208.

as well as other things in India."[3] Nehru thus offered his full co-operation with the Cabinet Mission.

The Cabinet Mission arrived in New Delhi on March 24. The ministers arrived in a mood of goodwill and this was declared by Pethick-Lawrence just after his arrival in India: "British Government and British people desire", announced Pethic Lawrence, "without reservation to consummate the promises and pledges that have been made and we can assure you that in our negotiations we shall not seek to provide anything that is incompatible in any way the sovereign dignity of India". The desire of the Mission was the desire of goodwill. He further continued: "We bring to the people of this country on behalf of the British Government and of the British people a message of cordial friendship and goodwill."[4] The Cabinet Mission thus represented the true intention of the British Government finally to solve the Indian problem. Initially Gandhiji had a favourable view to the Cabinet Mission. After four days of searching examination, he wrote in *Harijan* of May 26, that "it was the best document the British Government could have produced in the circumstances."[5]

True to their intention, the Mission was soon involved in the impossible task of maintaining the unity of India. The three ministers began lengthy discussions with the representatives of the political parties—the Congress and the League, the Princely States, the Sikhs, the Harijans and with Gandhiji. But there was no positive outcome of this talk, Jinnah remained firm on Pakistan, Congress and the League left to fight it out between themselves, while the Mission in utter perplexity[6], requested Gandhiji to keep in touch with them during the whole progress of the negotiations. Congress had some ideals before them and obviously it was in a disadvantageous position, pulled

3. *Ibid.*, p. 207.
4. S. I. N. C, II, pp. 791-792.
5. Nanda, B. R., Mahatma Gandhi—A Biography (London, 1958), p. 488.
6. Pethick Lawrence and Cripps were the supporters of the Congress, but they were held back by Wavell and Alexander.

in two different directions by its left and right wings, while Jinnah was the sole exponent of the League. Thus Congress could not act decisively and swiftly. Gandhiji was now too old and virtually after 1942, he had renounced the leadership. Nehru was temparamentally unsuitable to plan ways and means of the two warring groups; while Patel a more practical one, stood second in the leadership of the Congress.

When the mutual distrust and misunderstanding ate up the vitality of the two contending parties, Pethick Lawrence tried once more to brush up their differences by declaring: "While the Congress are representative of larger numbers... (than the League) it would not be right to regard the......League as merely a minority," At the same time, he furthor reminded the announcement of Attlee: "I am well aware, when I speak of India, that I speak of a country containing a congeries of races, religions and languages..... We are very mindful of the rights of minorities (who) should be able to live free from fear. On the other hand, we cannot allow a minority to place a veto on the advance of the majority." As the freedom of India was the goal of the Cabinet Mission, Pethick Lawrence further reminded the announcement of the British Prime Minister by stating that if India wanted independence "it will be for us to help to make the transition as smooth and easy as possible."[7]

The Cabinet Mission made it clear their purpose of visit before the Indian leaders, for setting out "to reconstitute the Viceroy's Executive Council as Coalition Interim Government," as well as "to secure agreement on the setting up of a constitution making body," The Mission also furthar clarified their scheme which was designed to give the Muslims the advantages of Pakistan without the disadvantages of dividing the country,[8] So to avoid this problem, the Mission proposed a constitution structure in three tiers, consisting of a Union, Groups and Provinces.

The union would consist of a Government and a Legislature. It would deal with Foreign Affairs, Defence and

7. Lumby, *Transfer of Power*, p. 72.
8. *Ibid*, pp. 80–81.

Communications besides the finance required for the purpose. All the remaining powers would vest in the Provinces. An intermediate tier might be formed by Provinces joining themselves into Groups, which might set up their own administration, Executives and Legislatures. The Groups were to decide which of the Provincial subjects they would take in common. Each Province might reconsider the terms of the constitution at the end of ten years. The essence of the compromise was the option to form Groups. By forming this scheme the Mission hoped that they would be able to persuade the League that if the Muslim Provinces could organise a Group, there would be no need of fear of extinction under the pressure of the Hindu majority.[9]

When there was no agreement among the members of the two major Indian parties, the Cabinet Mission began speculation how to avoid the Simla farce of July 1945. In a statement Pethick-Lawrence said: "We have come but with one purpose in view. It is, in conjunction with Lord Wavell, to discuss with the leaders of India and her elected representatives how best to speed the fulfilment of your aspirations to take full control of your own affairs and thus enable us to complete the transfer of responsibility".[10] Thus, to arrive at a formal agreement, the Cabinet Mission invited the Congress and the League to select four delegates each to meet at a Conference at Simla: "The Cabinet Mission and His Excellency the Viceroy have carefully reviewed the opinion expressed to them by the various representatives they have interviewed[11] and have come to the conclusion that they should make one further attempt to obtain agreement between the Muslim League and the Congress," wrote Pethick-Lawrence on April 27, to Maulana Abul Kalam Azad, the President of the Congress, and requested him to send the name of four Congress

9. Dorothy, *Nehru*, II, p. 226,
10, S. I. N. C., II, p. 792.
11. The members of the Cabinet Mission interviewed no less than 472 leaders from different parties.

delegates to negotiate at Simla.[12] He wrote similar letter to the Muslim League as well.

The Working Committee of the Congress agreed with the Cabinet Mission to be held at Simla, but also at the same time, sent its own proposals: "We have envisaged a Federal Union of autonomous units. Such a Federal Union must of necessity deal with certain essential subjects of which defence and its allied subjects are the most important, It must be organic and must have both an executive and legislative machinery as well as the finance relating to these subjects." About the formation of Groups of the Provinces, the Working Committee further observed: "We consider it wrong to form groups of Provinces under the Federal Union and more so on religious or communal basis." While the Congress agreed that the Provinces would have full powers in regard to all remaining subjects but at the same time, "it should be open to any province to exercise its option to have more common subjects with the Federal Union." The Congress become "ready to carry on negotiations with any party" and sent the name of four delegates—Abul Kalam Azad, Jawaharlal Nehru, Ballabhbhai Patel and Khan Abdul Ghaffar Khan[13], to take part in the proposed Simla Conference.

The Working Committee of the Muslim League also agreed to participate in the Conference but at the same time, its President reminded the Mission about the Muslim League's firm stand on the Lahore resolution of 1940.[14] "Therefore", the President wrote to Pethick-Lawrence, "without prejudice or commitment", the League wanted to assist the Mission in finding out "an agreed solution" of Indian constitutional problem by sending the four names, M. A. Jinnah, Mohammad

12. Letter from Pethick-Lawrence to Maulana Abdul Kalam Azad, April 27, 1946 (*Ibid.*, p. cxlviii).
13. Abul Kalam Azad's letter to Pethick-Lawrence, April 28, 1946.
14. In the Lahore session, held on March 23, 1940, the Muslim League for the first time, made a resolution for Pakistan on the basis of 'Two-Nation' theory.

Ismail Khan, Liaqat Ali Khan and Abdur Rab Nishtar,[15] to participate in the proposed Conference. But at the same time, the President also enclosed the resolution of the League held on April 9, 1946.

The enclosed resolution of the Muslim League demonstrated : "Whereas in this vast sub-continent of India a hundred million Muslims are the adherents of the Faith which regulates every department of their life (educational, social, economic and political), whose code is not confined merely to spiritual doctrines and tenets or rituals and ceremonies and which stands in sharp contrast to the exclusive nature of Hindu Dharma and Philosophy which has fostered and maintained for thousands of years a rigid caste system resulting in the degradation of 60 million human beings." The resolution further observed that even in a United Indian Federation, the interests of the Muslims would not be adequately protected. Therefore the League proposed a separate state of Pakistan by observing : "Whereas the Muslims are convinced that with a view to save Muslim India from the domination of the Hindus and in order to afford them full scope to develop themselves according to their genius, it is necessary to constitute a sovereign independent state comprising Bengal and Assam in the North-East Zone and the Punjab, North-West Frontier Province, Sind and Baluchistan in the North-West Zone."[16]

Pethick-Lawrence in his reply to the Congress President clarified the scope and intention of the proposed conference observing that the Mission did not think "that acceptance by Congress and the Muslim League for our invitation would imply as a preliminary condition full approval by them of the terms set out in my letter. These terms are our proposed basis for a settlement." However he hoped that the Congress representatives would arrive at Simla in time to open the discussion on the morning of May 2. Similar letter he wrote

15. Letter from Jinnah to Pethick Lawrence, April 29, 1946.
16. Resolution of the Muslim League, April 9, 1946 (vide, S. I. N. C, II, pp. cl-cli.

to the President of the Muslim League as well to take part in the proposed Conference, adding that Gandhiji had been requested by the Working Committee of the Congress, as well as by the Cabinet Mission to proceed to Simla.[17] Thus Gandhiji attended the Conference as a special invitee.

SIMLA CONFERENCE : May 5-12, 1946

The Simla Conference started from May 5, instead of the schedule day on May 2[18], where besides the representatives of the Congress and the League, the Cabinet delegation as well as the Viceroy took part in deliberations.

On the very first day of the Conference, the two warring groups, the Congress and the League, were not prepared to accept the viewpoint of other ; neither the Cabinet Mission could put forward a basis for agreement. The approach of the Congress had largely been ignored. The Congress had already made it clear that there can be no independence so long there would remain a foreign army in India. Congress stood for the independence of the whole of India. The discussion on 'A Constituent Assembly' in the Conference vexed the Congress, which according to it "is not going to decide the question of independence" and it had to be decided in the Conference. Neither the Constituent Assembly was "bound by any previous arrangements." On the very first day, repeated references were also made to "Groups" of provinces having an executive and legislative machinery. The method of grouping had not been discussed by the Congress beforehand and as such the Congress President alleged : "We are entirely opposed to any executive or legislative mechinery for a group of provinces or units of the Federation." This arrangement would create three layers of executive and legislative bodies, resulting in continuous friction. The Congress emphatically pointed out

17. Letter from Pethick-Lawrence to the Presidents of the Congress and the League, April 29, 1946 (vide, *Ibid.*, pp. cli-clii).
18. Muller, Edmund and Bhattacharjee, Arun, *India Wins Independencc* (New Delhi, 1988), p. 152.

that the Conference had no right "to entertain any suggestions for a division of India." Congress also did not accept the proposal of parity. The question of parity went "against the basic principles of democracy,"[19] the President alleged.

When the Congress could not meet the demands of the League, the Cabinet Mission suggested some further points of possible agreement. As a concession to the Congress, the original list of the Union subjects concerning only Foreign Affairs, Defence and Communications might be enlarged by the addition of Fundamental Rights and the Union Government might obtain for itself the finances it required for those subjects. To make the Union acceptable to the League it was suggested to divide the Constituent Assembly into three sections, one representing the Hindu-majority Provinces, the second representing the Muslim-majority Provinces and the third representing the States. The first two sections would meet separately and decide the Provincial Constitutions for their respective groups. To avoid the compulsory grouping of provinces in a particular section, it was proposed that a province might opt out of the original group or to choose another group or to remain out of any group by a majority of votes. The three sections would then meet together to frame the Union constitution.[20]

According to this proposal of the Cabinet Mission, there would thus be three sub-federations under the Union Constitution ; one for Hindu-majority provinces, another for the Muslims and the third for the States. The Muslim-majority provinces would have a parity of representation in the Union Legislature as well as in the Union Government with the Hindu majority Provinces. To compensate the League for the possible loss, through opting out of the North-Western Frontier Province from the Muslim-majority group, it was proposed that no measure affecting a communal issue in the Union Consti-

19. S. I. N. C., II, p. clviii.
20. Pyarelal, Mahatma Gandhi—the Last Phase, Vol. I, (Ahmedabad, 1956), pp. 205-208 ; also quoted in Dorothy, *Nehru* II, pp. 226–227.

tution would be passed unless the majority of both the major communities voted in its favour.[21]

On May 8, the Cabinet Mission suggested some of the following main points of agreement between the two contending parties :

A : "There shall be an All-India Union Government and Legislature dealing with Foreign Affairs, Defence, Communications, Fundamental Rights and having the necessary powers to obtain for itself the finances it requires for these subjects.

"Groups of Provinces may be formed and such groups may determine the Provincial subjects which they desire to take in common.

"The Legislature of the Union shall be composed of equal proportions from the Muslim-majority Provinces and from the Hindu-majority Provinces whether or not these or any of them have formed themselves into groups together with representatives of the States.

"The Constitution of the Union and the groups (if any) shall contain a provision whereby any Province can by a majority of vote of its legislative assembly call for a reconsideration of the terms of the Constitution after an initial period of 10 years and at 10 yearly intervals thereafter,

B : "The Constitution-making machinery to arrive at a Constitution on the above basis shall be as follows :

"Representatives shall be elected from each Provincial Assembly in proportion to the strengths of the various parties in that assembly on the basis of 1/10th of their numbers.

"Representatives shall be invited from the States on the basis of their population in proportion to the representation from British India.

21. *Ibid.*, p. 227.

> "After its preliminary meeting at which the general order of business shall be settled it will divide into three sections, one section representing the Hindu-majority Provinces, one section representing the Muslim-majority Provinces and one representing the States.
>
> "The First two sections will then meet separately to decide the Provincial constitutions for their group and, if they wish, a group constitution.
>
> "When these have been settled it will be open to any Province to decide to opt out of its original groups and into the another group or to remain outside any group.
>
> "Thereafter the three bodies will meet together to settle the constitution for the Union on the lines agreed.
>
> "No major point in the Union constitution which affects the communal issue shall be deemed to be passed by the Assembly unless a majority of both the two major communities vote into its favour.[22]

Muslim League became out of temper when they received this proposal stating that "the Congress finally and definitely turned down the proposed Union confined only to three subjects even with power to levy contribution for financing the Union." The League further pressed for two constitution-making bodies instead of one complaining that "the new suggested points for agreement are a fundamental departure from the original formula" of the Cabinet Mission. Thus the League did not agree for "a single constitution making body."[23]

While the negotiations with the Cabinet Mission and the League was in progress in Simla, Azad's Presidentship of the Congress came to an end and when he had declined to continue for a second term, Nehru's name was proposed for the President

22. S. I. N. C., II, pp. cliv- clv.
23. *Ibid*,, pp. clv–clvi,

of the Congress on May 9.[24] But Azad was requested to continue till Nehru would resume the office. From this time Nehru became the mouthpice of the Congress once again, with the responsibility of solving the problem of Indian independence at such a critical situation against the hostile attitude of the League. On the very outset, he vehemently criticised the Secretary of State by stating that his suggestions were entirely opposed to the views of the Congress. It was the desire of the Congress to explore every avenue for a settlement but there was certain point of limits beyond which the Congress could not proceed, The Congress wanted a strong and organic Federal Union against sub-federations or grouping of provinces. Similarly the Congress wholly opposed the question of parity. "The only reasonable course appears to us," wrote Nehru to Pethick-Lawrence, "is to have a Constituent Assembly with perfect freedom to draw up its constitution, with certain reservations to protect the rights of minorities," He further wrote: "There is also compulsion in the early stages for a Province to join a particular group whether it wants to or not." He then challenged the validity by stating, "why should the Frontier Province, which is clearly a Congress Province, be compelled to join any group hostile to the Congress?"[25]

The Congress was prepared to accept the formation of groups if it was entirely optional. The Congress advocated that this would be for the representatives of the Provinces to decide after the framing of the Constituent Assembly for the All-India Federal Union. The League, on the other hand, demanded from the very beginning a separate constitution-making body for the six Muslim Provinces, namely, the Punjab, the North-Western Frontier Province, Baluchistan, Sind, Bengal and Assam.[26] After the completion of the Constitution of the

24. Brecher, Michael, *Nehru : A Political Biography* (London, 1959), p. 314.
25. S. I. N. C., II, pp. clvii-clviii.
26. The Muslim League claimed Assam, although it was a Hindu-majority Province.

Pakistan Federal Government, the Constitution-making bodies of the two groups—the Pakistan group and the Hindustan group might sit together to deal with the three subjects only, Foreign Affairs, Defence and 'Communications necessary for Defence.'[27]

There were other points of difference. The Congress wanted the Union Government to have the power to raise the finances ; the League insisted that the Federal Union should in no event have the power to raise revenues in its own rights but only by contribution. Whereas the Congress agreed to optional grouping of Provinces and a Muslim veto "in order to allay the anxiety of the Muslims, so that Hindus and Muslims might be able to live together as one nation in their common motherland." Muslims vehemently protested against it for their cherished goal of Pakistan. The Congress feared, from the very beginning, the difficulty about parity in regard to the executive or the legislature, comprising a population of nineteen crores of the Hindu-majority Provinces, as against a little over of nine crores of Muslim-majority Provinces. In disgust Gandhiji wrote to Cripps on May 8 : "This is worse than Pakistan." As a way out of it, he suggested that "an impartial non-British tribunal should make an award on this issue" in case of any difference, did not ultimately materialise. The Congress was ready to do anything within the bounds of reason to remove fear and suspicion from the mind of the minority-community, but not at the cost of its basic method of democracy, on which the Congress wanted to build up a Constitution. Nehru's suggestion for the appointment of an umpire, in case of difference between the two contending parties, was also turned down by the Muslim League.[28]

On the last day of the Conference at Simla, the President of the Muslim League submitted a memorandum before the Cabinet Mission embodying their minimum demands :

27. Dorothy, *Nehru*, II, p. 227.
28. Pyarelal, *Mahatma Gandhi*, I, pp. 205-208.

"The six Muslim Provinces (Punjab, N. W. F. P., Baluchistan, Sind, Bengal and Assam) shall be grouped together as one group and will deal with all other subjects and matters except Foreign Affairs, Defence and communications necessary for Defence, which may be dealt with by the Constitution-making bodies of the two groups of Provinces—Muslim Provinces (hereinafter named Pakistan group) and Hindu Provinces—sitting together.

"There shall be a separate Constitution-making body for the six Muslim Provinces named above, which will frame Constitutions for the Group and the Provinces in the Group and will determine the list of subjects that shall be Provinciai and Central (of the Pakistan Federation) with residuary sovereign powers vesting in the Provinces.

"After the Constitutions of the Pakistan Federal Government and the Provinces are finally framed by the Constitution-making body, it will be open to any Province of the Group to decide to opt out of its Group, provided the wishes of the people of that Province are ascertained by referendum to opt out or not.

"It must be open to discussion in the joint Constitution-making body as to whether the Union will have a Legislature or not. The method of providing the Union with finance should also be left for decision of the joint meeting of the two Constitution-making bodies, but in no event shall it be by means of taxation,

"There should be parity of representation between the two Groups of Provinces in the Union Executive and the Legislature, if any.

"No major point in the Union Constitution which affects the communal issue shall be deemed to be passed in the joint Constitution-making body, of the Hindu Provinces and the majority of the members of the Constitution-making body of the Pakistan Group, present and voting, are separately in its favour.

"No decision, legislative, executive or administrative, shall be taken by the Union in regard to any matter of controversial nature, except by a majority of three-fourths.

"The Constitution of the Union shall contain a provision whereby any Province can, by a majority vote of its Legislative Assembly, call for reconsideration of the terms of the Constitution, and will have the liberty to sceede from the Union at any time after an initial period of ten years."[29]

Jawaharlal Nehru also, on behalf of the Congress, suggested the following points as a basis for agreement :

"Constitution Assembly to be formed as follows :

1. Representatives shall be elected by each Provincial Assembly by proportional representation (single transferable vote). The number so elected shouid be one-fifth of the number of members of the Assembly.

2. Representatives from the States on the basis of their population in proportion to the representation from British India.

"The Constituent Assembly shall draw up a Constitution for the Federal Union. This shall consist of an All-India Federal Government and Legislature dealing with Foreign Affairs, Defence, Communications, Fundamental Rights, Currency, Customs and Planning......The Federal Union will have necessary powers to obtain for itself the finances it requires for these subjects and the power to raise revenues in its own rights

"All the remaining powers shall vest in the Provinces or Units.

"Groups of Provinces may be formed and such groups may determine the Provincial subjects which they desire to take in common.

29. Memorandum by the President of the Muslim League, May 12, 1946 (S. I. N C., II, pp. clx-clxi).

"After the Constituent Assembly has decided the Constitution for the All–India Federal Union .....the representatives of the Provinces may form groups to decide the Provincial Constitutions for their group, if they wish, a group Constitution.

"No major part in the All-India Federal Constitution which affects the communal issue shall be deemed to be passed by the Constituent Assembly unless a majority of members of the community or communities concerned present in Assembly and voting are separately in its favour, provided that in case there is no agreement on any such issue, it will be referred to arbitration. In case of doubt, as to whether any point is a major communal issue, the speaker will decide, or, if so desired, it may be referred to the Federal Court.

"In the event of a dispute arising in the process of Constitution-making the specific issue shall be referred to arbitration."[30]

As there was no basis of agreement regarding any major issue, such as Constitution-making, provisions of Union and Provincial Legislatures, Group, parity, Umpire and many other related points of importance between the Congress and the Muslim League, the Cabinet Mission was broke up on May 12, without achieving its objectives. Attlee announced the Mission's opposition to Jinnah's claim on partition. Wavell also favoured a United India. There was no approval of the British about Jinnah's demand "that the Muslim majority provinces should have full autonomy." Azad criticised this as the Muslim League's leaders loose talk of partitioning the country and thereby establishing an independent State of Pakistan.[31]

30. Points suggested by the Congress on the basis of Agreement, May 12 (S. I. N. C., II, pp. clxi–clxii).
31. About the Muslim League's claim of Pakistan, Azad reacted sharply stating that "it is harmful not only for India as a whole but for Muslims in particular .... The very term Pakistan goes against my grain .. The scheme of Pakistan is a symbol of defeatism"—Azad, I. W. F., pp. 150-152.

CABINET MISSION'S OWN PLAN, May 16

(A long term Constitutional Scheme)

After the failure of the Simla Conference the Cabinet Mission and the Viceroy moved down to Delhi and on May 16, issued a statement proposing to set up a Constitution-making body in India. When the agreement between the Congress and the League could not be reached at Simla, the Cabinet Mission tried once more to decide about the future Constitution of India. Now they tried to form an Interim-Government for the administration of British India until a new Constitution could be brought into being by declaring : "After prolonged discussions in New Delhi we succeeded in bringing the Congress and the Muslim League together in Conference at Simla. There was a full exchange of views and both parties were prepared to make considerable concessions in order to try and reach a settlement but it ultimately proved impossible to close the remainder of the gap between the parties and so no agreement could be concluded. Since no agreement has been reached we feel that it is our duty to put forward what we consider are the best arrangements possible to ensure a speedy setting up of the new Constitution."[32]

On the very outset the Mission rejected the idea of Pakisian "A separate sovereign state of Pakistan on the lines claimed by the Muslim League would not solve the communal minority problem." Therefore the Mission did not think it proper "to advise the British government that the power which at present resides in British hands should be handed over to two entirely sovereign states."[33] The Mission further claimed that they would provide Justice to both sections of the people, but at the same time, they could not underestimate the "genuine and acute anxiety of the Muslims lest they should find themselves subjected to a perpetual Hindu-majority rule." This feeling had become so strong and widespread among the

32. Statement by the Cabinet Delegation and the Viceroy, New Delhi, May 16, 1946.
33. Azad, I. W. F., pp. 150-151.

Muslims "that it cannot be allayed by mere paper safeguards."[34]

The Cabinet Delegation now began to examine about the validity of Muslim League's claim of creating a separate and sovereign Pakistan. Such a Pakistan, according to the League's demand was to comprise two areas; one in the North-West consisting of the Provinces of the Punjab, Sind, North-West Frontier, and Baluchistan; while the other in the north-east, consisting of the Provinces of Bengal and Assam. In case of Bengal and Assam, the League was prepared to consider adjustment of boundaries, but remained firm on the principle of Pakistan. The League's argument for a separate State of Pakistan was based on the right of the Muslims to decide their method of government according to their wishes. The six Provinces of the North-Western areas as claimed by the League constituted 62.07% of Muslim and 37.93% of non-Muslim population; whereas the North-eastern areas comprised 51.69% of the Muslims and 48.31% of non-Muslim population.[35] These figures showed that the claim of a separate sovereign State of Pakistan would not solve the communal minority problem. The Cabinet Delegation further argued that there was no "Justification for including within a sovereign Pakistan those districts of the Punjab and of Bengal and Assam in which the population is predominantly non-Muslim."

On the question of the partition of Bengal and the Punjab, where non-Muslim population were in considerable number, the Cabinet Delegation did not give their verdict in favour of partition. On this point, they argued: "We therefore considered whether a smaller sovereign Pakistan confined to the Muslim majority areas alone might be a possible basis of compromise. Such a Pakistan is regarded by the Muslim League as quite impracticable because it would entail the exclusion from Pakistan of (a) the whole of the Ambala and Jullundur Division in the Punjab; (b) the whole of Assam

34. S. I. N. C., II, p. clxiv,
35. Based on the Census of 1941.

except the district of Sylhet; and (c) a large part of Western Bengal, including Calcutta, in which city the Muslim form 23.6 per cent of the population. We Ourselves are also convinced that any solution which involves a radical partition of the Punjab and Bengal, as this would do, would be contrary to the wishes and interests of a very large proportion of the inhabitants of these Provinces. Bengal and the Punjab each has its common language and a long history and tradition. Moreover any division of the Punjab would of necessity divide the Sikhs leaving substantial bodies of Sikhs on both sides of the boundary." After making the observation, the Cabinet Delegation concluded: "We have therefore been forced to the conclusion that neither a larger nor a smaller sovereign State of Pakistan would provide an acceptable solution for the communal problem."[36]

The Cabinet Delegation also pointed out other difficulties that might arise by dividing the country. Besides the Hindus and the Muslim a greater difficulty might arise from the Indian States, who were to associate themselves, willingly or unwillingly, with a divided India. The case of two territories of Pakistan was also not easy to meet. The two halves of the proposed Pakistan, separated by hundreds of miles, "the communications between them both in war and peace would be dependent on the goodwill of Hindustan." Thus the demand for a larger Pakistan seemed unjustifiable and a smaller or truncated Pakistan seemed unfeasible to them.

The Cabinet Delegation therefore proposed, for the satisfaction of all parties, and for a stable and practicable form of Constitution for All-India, recommended mainly on three issues of importance in avoiding partition (a) A Union of India, (b) A Constitution-making body and (c) about the grouping of the Provinces. Their proposals were under the following basic form :

"There should be a Union of India, embracing both British India and the States, which should deal with the

36, S. I. N. C., II, p. clxv.

following subject: Foreign Affairs, Defence and Communications; and should have the powers necessary to raise the finances required for the above subjects.[37]

"The Union should have an Executive and a Legislature Constituted from British Indian and States representatives. Any question raising a major communal issue in the Legislature should require for its decision a majority of the representatives present and voting of each of the two major communities as well as a majority of all the members present and voting.

"All subjects other than the Union subjects and all residuary powers should vest in the Provinces.

"Provinces should be free to form Groups with executives and legislatures, and each Group could determine the Provincial subjects to be taken in common.

"The Constitutions of the Union and of the Groups should contain a provision whereby any Province could, by a majority vote of its Legislative Assembly, call for a reconsideration of the Terms of the Constitution after an initial period of 10 years and at 10 yearly intervals thereafter."[38]

At the same time, the Cabinet Delegation pointed out that the details of a constitution could be settled by Indians for Indians. They further proposed and framed out how the representatives from each Provincial Legislative Assembly would be elected by the method of proportional representation with a single transferable vote. For this purpose they divided the country into three zones, A, B and C, as the members of the Mission felt that this was to give a greater sense of assurance to the minorities.[39] Section A was to consist of Hindu-majority Provinces of Madras, Bombay, United Provinces, Bihar, Central Provinces and Orissa. Section B was to

---

37. Pethick-Lawrence wanted to include currency in the Central list but he left this matter to be decided later by the Constituent Assembly.
38. *Ibid.*, p. clxvi; also, ANM, p. 246.
39. Menon, V.P., *The Transfer of Power in India* (New Jersey, 1957), pp. 466-475.

consist of North-West Frontier Provinces, Punjab and Sind; while Section C was to consist of Bengal and Assam. The table of representation had been proposed as under :

Section-A

Province	General	Muslim	Total
Madras	45	4	49
Bombay	19	2	21
United Provinces	47	8	55
Bihar	31	5	36
Central Provinces	16	1	17
Orissa	9	0	9
Total	167	20	187

Section-B

	General	Muslim	Sikh	Total
North-West Frontier Province	0	3	0	3
Punjab	8	16	4	28
Sind	1	3	0	4
Total	9	22	4	35

Section-C

	General	Muslim	Total
Bengal	27	33	60
Assam	7	3	10
Total	34	36	70

Total for British India	292
Maximum for Indian States	93
Total	385

It was also proposed that the representatives from the Chief Commissioners Provinces, such as Delhi, Ajmer-Merwara and Coorg were to be added in Section A, while one representative from Baluchistan be added in Section B.[40]

40. ANM, p. 247 ; also, S. I. N. C., II, pp. clxvii–clxviii.

For the purpose of making a Constitution for free India, the representatives of the Provinces were to meet at New Delhi, to elect a Chairman, the other officers and an Advisory Committee for the same purpose.[41] Then the Provincial representatives were to divide up into three separate sections in accordance with the grouping of the Provinces.[42] The three sections were then to proceed to settle the Provincial Constitutions for their respective Provinces and were to decide whether any group Constitution was to be set up for these Provinces. They were to select the lists of Provincial subjects to deal with. Similarly, no directive was laid down for the States' representatives, but they were to reassemble with the Provincial representatives. In case of any major communal issue, the Union Constituent Assembly was to decide by a majority of the representatives present and voting of each of the two major communities. Then the Chairman of the Assembly, in consultation with the Federal Court, was to decide the issue.

There was also a provision for a province of a particular group to withdraw from that group and select another group, but it could be possible only after the Union Constitution had been framed, as well as the elections to the Union and Provincial legislatures had been completed.[43] After an initial period of ten years and at ten-yearly intervals, any Province, by a majority of vote, could call for a reconsideration of the terms of the Union or Group Constitution.[44]

While Constitution-making was to proceed on these lines, the Viceroy was to form an Interim-Government with the

41. The Advisory Committee was to contain full representatives of the interest affected and they were to report and advise the Union Constituent Assembly the rights of the tribal and minorities.
42. For example, the representatives from Bengal and Assam were to form one group.
43. For example, if Assam, a Hindu-majority Province wanted to withdraw from Section C, where the majority representatives was bound to be Muslims, it could do so only after its constitution had been settled at a sectional meeting.
44. S. I. N. C., II, p. clxviii.

support of the major political parties. It was essential during this interim period, of maximum co-operation in carrying through the difficult task ahead, besides the heavy task of day to day administration. "To the leaders of the people of India," declared the Cabinet Mission in a statement, "who now have the opportunity of complete independence we would finally say that we and our Government and countrymen hope that it would be possible for the Indian people themselves to agree upon the method of framing the new Constitution under which they live." Two days after this announcement, Pethick-Lawrence made a separate broadcast for the people of India : "The words which I shall speak to you are concerned with the future of a great people—the people of India. There is a passionate desire in the hearts of Indians expressed by the leaders of all their political parties for independence. His Majesty's Government and the British people as a whole are fully ready to accord this independence whether within or without the British Commonwealth and hope that out of it will spring a lasting and friendly association between our two peoples on a footing of complete equality."[45] Pethick-Lawrence also made it clear, while meeting at a Press Conference that the Mission had not announced an award. It was only a recommendation to certain basic principles of the Constitution and a decision to invite Indian representatives to make their own Constitution. So there was no question of enforcing an award.

The British government repeatedly assured the Indian people of their good intention of granting independence to India. The British Commander-in-Chief made a broadcast, just after the Mission's announcement, about their attempt to find out a suitable agreement to the Congress and the League, but no agreement had been reached at Simla. The possibility of setting up a separate State of Pakistan had been carefully examined by the Cabinet Delegation, but finally came to a conclusion "that the setting up of completely independent

45 Broadcast of Pethick-Lawrence. May 17 (Vide, *Ibid.*, p. clxx,)

states not linked together in any way would not result in a settlement of the differences between the Hindu and Muslim," which might result "great loss and danger to India in the future." He further argued about the decision of British government for such a step: "The British Government, therefore, have approved neither the setting up of completely separate States nor the retention of all power at the Centre. They consider that although the different areas should have a large measure of independence if the people desire it, the responsibility for the Army, Navy and Air Force and for the defence of the whole of India in War, must rest with one authority for the whole of India."[46]

The reaction of the Congress towards the announcement of May 16 was not favourable. They were hesitant to accept the proposals until some clarifications were made before joining the Constituent Assembly or formation of the Interim Government. The Congress Working Committee, after carefully examining the proposals came to a decision that the formation of a Provisional Government and the clarification given by the members of the Delegation, were incomplete and vague. Thus about the formation of the Provisional Government at the centre, the Congress Working Committee resolved on May 24: "The Committee regret to find divergence between these objectives and the various proposals that have been made on behalf of the British Government, and, in particular, there is no vital change envisaged during the interim period when the Provisional Government will function..... If the independence of India is aimed at, then...... all obstructions and hindrances to it should be removed. The continued presence of a foreign army of occupation is a negation of independence." So far as the building up of a Constituent Assembly was concerned, the Committee did not agree with some of the recommendations of the Mission. The Congress viewed the Constituent Assembly, a sovereign body, but at any stage this

46. The Broadcast of the Commander-in-Chief, May 17 (vide, *Ibid.*, p. clxxxi.)

Assembly could be subjected to change and variations if the proposals of the Mission were accepted. Moreover such an Assembly would not get full representations from all Provincial Legislatures.[47] On the question of 'Provincial autonomy', and 'Provincial Constitutions', the Congress opined that there was 'a marked discrepancy' in these two separate provisions that might result in compulsory grouping of the Provinces and the introduction of such compulsion "clearly infringes the basic principle of provincial autonomy." In order to retain the recommendatory character of the Mission's proposals and to make the clauses consistent with each other the Congress interpreted the recommendations in its own way. Thus according to the interpretation of the Congress, the Provinces were to select, at first, whether or not they belonged to a particular section in which they were placed. "Thus the Constituent Assembly must be considered as a sovereign body with final authority for the purpose of drawing up a constitution and giving effect to it," the Congress Working Committee observed in their note. They also further pointed out about the shortcomings of the proposals by stating that the Cabinet Delegation did not make their policy clear about the Indian States.[48] The Congress also criticised about the method of formation of a Provisional National Government, which must be a precursor of full independence that was to emerge from the Constituent Assembly. The Governor-General might continue as the head of the government during the interim period, "but the Government should function as a Cabinet responsible to the Central Legislature. The Status, powers and composition of the Provisional Government should be fully defined in order to enable the Committee to come to a decision." The Congress believed that a Provisional Government

47. In Baluchistan there was no elected assembly. It would be improper, the Congress viewed with concern, to nominate anyone to speak on behalf of the whole Province of Baluchistan.

48. The Congress suggested that the manner of appointing State representatives for the Constituent Assembly must approximate, to the method adopted in the Provinces.

and a Constituent Assembly should be viewed together, as if they were the parts of the same picture, with the conviction that they were engaged in building up a free and independent India. "In the absence of a full picture," the Congress observed in its concluding note, "the Committee are unable to give a final opinion at this stage."[49]

The Congress after vehemently criticising the proposals, wanted to know the actual position of the Interim-Government. During these critical days before assuming power, a large number of letters had been exchanged between the Congress President and the Viceroy–Wavell. On behalf of the Congress, Azad wrote to Wavell to raise the status of the Interim-Government, without which it "would not be in a position to infuse in the Indian people a consciousness of freedom." The Congress believed that after the British Government's declaration then "the Constituent Assembly will be the final authority for framing the Constitution and any Constitution framed by it will be binding, the recognition of Indian independence is imminent." At the same time the Congress also wanted the assurance "that the Interim Government would in practice functions like a Dominion Cabinet." The Congress believed that if the questions of status and responsibility of the Interim–Government were satisfactorily solved, the Congress "would be able to decide other questions without any delay,"[50] In replying the letter of Azad, the Viceroy sharply denied that the Interim Government was to have the same powers as a Dominion Cabinet. The British had the intention of allowing the Interim Government "the greatest possible freedom in the exercise of day to day administration of the country," if it could faithfully carry out the purpose behind it. He believed that the spirit of working in a government was of much greater importance "than any formal document and guarantee."[51]

49. S. I. N. C., II, pp. cxcix–cci.
50. Letter from Azad to Wavell, May 25.
51. Wavell's letter to Azad, May 30.

But on these assurances, the Congress was not fully satisfied about the status and powers of the Interim Government that the British professed. From Ahmedabad, Gandhiji also raised objection on this point of the Provisional Government and described it a vital defect. Writing in *Harijan*, Gandhiji observed : "The question of Paramountcy is unsolved. It is not enough to say that Paramountcy will end with the end of British rule in India. If it persists without check during the Interim period, it will have behind a difficult legacy for the independent Government." He further observed by concluding : "The acid test is that it should be able to stand alone, erect and unbending, During the interim period we must learn to hop unaided, if we are to walk when we are free."[52]

But the reaction of the Muslim League to Cabinet Mission's proposals was different. At first Jinnah was completely opposed to the scheme but after some days he "admitted that there could be no fairer solution of the minority problem than that presented in the Cabinet Mission Plan." He told the League's council that the scheme presented by the Cabinet Mission was the maximum that he could secure. As such, Jinnah advised the Muslim League to accept the scheme and the League agreed unanimously in its favour.[53] Thus when came to know about League's attitude, Wavell offered the League and the Congress, on June 3, "equal representation" in the proposed Interim Government,[54] the League accepted the invitation with certain clarifications of getting assurance on the question of Parity. Wavell assured Jinnah, on behalf of Cabinet Delegation, his personal assurance : "We do not propose to make any discrimination in the treatment of either parity and that we shall go ahead with the Plan laid down in the statement."[55] But as the Congress could not make any decision, Jinnah was not in a hurry to adjust the portfolios. In his letter Jinnah further stated that "no use or purpose would

52. *Harijan*, 2. 6. 1946.
53. Azad, I. W. F., pp. 175-176.
54. Wavell added two more members, one representing the Sikhs, the other untouchables.
55. Letter from Wavell to Jinnah, June 4.

be saved until the Congress have given their decision with regard to the scheme embodied in the statement of the Mission of May 16."[56]

After Jinnah's consent in the formation of Interim Government, Wavell invited Nehru to fill up various portfolios, reminding at the same time, that there was no question of parity, but to concentrate on the common objective in forming "the last possible Interim Government drawn from the two major parties and some of the minorities." But the Working Committee of the Congress rejected the suggestion of joining in the Interim Government. It was due to the principle of 'parity' with the League for which the Congress entirely opposed the scheme from the very beginning. The Congress President argued the reasons for declining the offer : "In the composition of the Cabinet suggested by you there is 'parity' between the Hindus including the scheduled castes and the Muslim League, that is the number of caste Hindus is actually less than the nominees of the Muslim League. The position thus is worse than it was in June 1945 at Simla where, according to your consideration then, there was to be 'parity' batween caste Hindus and Muslims, leaving additional seats for the Scheduled Caste Hindus. The Muslim seats then were not reserved for the Muslim League only but could include non-League Muslims. The present proposal thus puts the Hindus in a very unfair position and at the same time eliminates the non-League Muslims. My Committee are not prepared to accept any such proposal." About the Viceroy's suggestions of solving the major communal issues by separate group voting, the Congress President remarked : "While we have accepted this principle for long-term arrangements, we did so as an effective substitute for other safeguards." But the present proposal of 'parity' with the growth of the convention of communal issue was to "make the working of the Provisional Government almost impossible and deadlock is certainty." To carry on the work of the Interim Government

56. Letter from Jinnah to Wavell, June 12.

efficiently, as well as to create somewhat a strong centre, the Congress President suggested: "The work before the Provisional Government is likely to be much heavier.... In your proposals communications include railways, transport, posts, telegraphs and air. It is difficult for us to conceive how all these can be joined together in one portfolio ... We think also that Planning is an essential department for the centre. We think, therefore, that the Provisional Government must consist of fifteen members." The Congress believed that for successful working of the coalition government some common outlook and programme must be adopted.[57]

On the next day, the Congress President again intimated Wavell about his resentment on 'parity'. The Congress considered it a dangerous innovation which, instead of working for harmony, was to be a source of constant conflict and trouble. It was to poison the future of India. Though it was a temporary arrangement, "but no such assurance can prevent an evil step from having evil consequences,"[58] the President remarked emphatically.

In reply to this Wavell stated that the statement of May 16 did not make grouping compulsory, which was to be decided by the elected representatives of the concerning Provinces sitting together in sections. It was decided that the representatives of certain provinces were to meet in sections to decide whether they wished to form groups. Even the individual Provinces had the liberty to opt out of a group if they so decided. On the question of 'parity', the Viceroy replied that six Congressmen and five Muslim Leagues besides the Viceroy himself, were to constitute the Interim Government, which could not be called 'parity'.[59]

The Cabinet Delegation and the Viceroy then realised that they could not bring about an agreed basis for the formation of

57. Letter from the Congress President to Wavell, June 13 (vide, S. I. N. C., II, pp. ccviii–ccix).
58. Letter from the Congress President to Wavell, June 14.
59. Letter from Wavell to the Congress President, June 15,

an Interim Government, at last issued a statement on June 16, setting forth their own proposal for the establishment of an Interim Government.

STATEMENT BY CABINET MISSION AND VICEROY JUNE 16

"His Excellency the Viceroy, in consultation with the members of the Cabinet Mission, has for some time been exploring the possibilities of forming a coalition Government drawn from the two major parties and certain of the minorities. The discussions have revealed the difficulties which exist for the two major parties in arriving at any agreed basis for the formation of such a Government.

"The Viceroy and the Cabinet Mission appreciate these difficulties and the efforts which the two parties have met to meet them. They consider, however, that no useful purpose can be served by further prolonging these discussions. It is indeed urgently necessary that a strong and representative Interim Government should be set up to conduct the very high and important business that has to be carried through.

"The Viceroy is therefore issuing invitations to the following to serve as members of the Interim Government on the basis that the Constitution-making will proceed in accordance with the Statement of May 16 :

Sardar Baldev Singh	Dr. Rajendra Prasad
Sir N. P. Engineer	Mr. H. K. Mahtab
Mr. Jagjivan Ram	Dr. John Mathai
Pandit Jawaharlal Nehru	Nawab Mohammad Ismail Khan
Mr. M. A. Jinnah	Khwaja Sir Nazimuddin
Nawabzada Liaquat Ali Khan	Sardar Abdub Rab Nishtar
Mr. C. Rajagopalachari	Sardar Vallabhbhai Patel

If any of those invited is unable for personal reasons to accept, the Viceroy will, after consultation, invite some other person in his place.

"The Viceroy will arrange the distribution of portfolios in consultation with the leaders of the two major parties.

"The Viceroy and the Cabinet Mission believe that Indians of all communities desire to arrive at a speedy settlement of this matter so that the process of Constitution-making can go forward and that the Government of India may be carried on as efficiently as possible in the meantime.

"They therefore hope that all parties especially the two major parties will accept this proposal so as to overcome the present obstacles, and will co-operate for the successful carrying on the Interim Government. Should this proposal be accepted, the Viceroy will aim at inaugurating the new Government about the 26th June.

"In the event of the two major parties or either of them proving unwilling to join the setting up of a coalition Government on the above lines, it is the intention of the Viceroy to proceed with the formation of an Interim Government which will be as representative as possible of those willing to accept the Statment of May 16th.

"The Viceroy is also directing the Governors of the Provinces to summon the Provincial Legislative Assemblies forthwith to proceed with the elections necessary for the setting up of the Constitution-making machinery as put forward in the Statement of May 16th."[60]

The Congress Working Committee subsequently considered the Cabinet Mission's statement of June 16, objected to one name out of the League's list of five, namely Abdul Rab Nishtar, but the objection was overruled. The Congress then made another objection of replacing the name of Sarat Chandra Bose by that of H. K. Mehtab. The Congress became further aggrieved for ignoring the names of Mrs. Amrit Kaur, Zakir Hussain and Muniswami Pillay. Thus the Congress had put forward their three objections, namely, the selection of

60. Quoted in Dorothy, *Nehru* II, pp. 232–233. Also, S. I. N. C., II, pp. ccxiii–ccxiv.

Nishtar from the North-West Frontier Province where he had been defeated in the election against a Congress candidate. Secondly, the omission of a nationalist or Congress Muslim[61] and thirdly, the changes that had been made without consulting the Congress.

When all these objections of the Congress had been overruled by the Viceroy, the Congress was put in a very difficult position. Still on June 18, a tentative decision was taken to accept the scheme of the Interim Government, as was emerged then. Struck with a sense of helplessness, Nehru went to Kashmir, to interfere in the politics of that state. In consequence of the Quit Kashmir Movement, Sheikh M. Abdullah—the President of the Kashmir National Conference was arrested on May 20 by the Kashmiri Government on trial for treason. The situation in Kashmir was a delicate one as the ruler of the state was a Hindu Hari Singh, the population was predominantly Muslim and the leader of the mass movement was a Muslim. Nehru being a Kashmiri himself, besides the Congress support for the State's people, was the only effective means of preventing the princes withdrawing from the Indian union. Without listening the advice of some of his friends,[62] as well as against the wishes of Wavell, Nehru decided to fly to Kashmir on June 19 for supporting Abdullah. But on the Kashmir border he was stopped by the State police who made Nehru under home arrest on June 20.[63] During this time the Congress was in crisis at Delhi, for they had to decide the Cabinet Mission's proposals of June 16. Azad and Patel requested Nehru to return immediately, while Wavell sent a special plane for him, and he forthwith returned to Delhi on June 22.

Within three days of Nehru's return, Congress decided to accept the long-term arrangement of May 16 reluctantly and to join the proposed Constituent Assembly; while it rejected the offer

61. At this critical moment Gandhiji intervened decisively. Congress being a National party, could not, in his view, agree to the omission of a Congress Muslim from the Interim Government.
62. Some people believed, particularly the Hindu Mahasabha as well as the right wing of the Congress that Abdullah was trying to drag Kashmir into the North-Western Pakistan zone.
63. Dorothy, *Nehru*, II, p. 233.

of June 16, declining to join the Interim Government. The Congress drafted their resolution accordingly : "The Congress, as you are aware, is a national organisation, including in its fold the members of all religions and communities in India . . It is from this point of view that we have to judge every proposal. We hoped that a Provisional National Government would be formed which would give effect in practice to this independence.... In this connection we emphasised that we could not accept anything in the nature of 'parity' even as a temporary expedient and pointed out that the Provisional Government should consist of fifteen members to enable the administration of the country to be carried on efficiently." The Congress also criticised the non-inclusion of any nationalist Muslim. Reacting sharply on this issue the Working Committee of the Congress wrote to Wavell observing : "You told us that the Cabinet Mission and you were not prepared to accept a request for the inclusion of a Muslim chosen by the Congress among the representatives of the Congress in the Interim Government. This seemed to us an extraordinary decision. It was in direct opposition to your own statement.... It meant that the Congress could not freely choose even its own nominees..... In the circumstances your proposals cannot fulfil the immediate requirements of the situation." While concluding the statement, the Congress further observed : "My Committee have, therefore, reluctantly come to the conclusion that they are unable to assist you in forming a Provisional Government, "but with regard to the proposals relating to the formation of the Constitution-making body, "we accept your proposals and are prepared to work them with a view to achieve our objective.[64]

The Viceroy became disappointed, but still the Cabinet Mission hoped that the talks between the leaders of the two parties regarding the formation of an Interim Government might be resumed after a brief interval. Thus in a letter to the Congress President, Wavell observed : "The Cabinet Delegation and I very much regret that the Congress Working Committee have not been able to accept the proposals... The Delegation and I are, however, glad to learn from the last paragraph of your letter that the

64. Letter from the Congress President to Wavell, June 25 (quoted in S. I. N. C., II, pp. ccxx-ccxxii).

Congress Working Committee accept, and are prepared to work, the proposals for framing a Constitution for India". As the negotiations in forming the Interim Government had failed, "it would be desirable to have a short interval before the matter is taken up again". Therefore the Viceroy decided "to form a Caretaker Government of officials to carry on the administration temporarily;"[65] while the election of the representatives of the Constituent Assembly was to go ahead.

Jinnah became greatly outraged when he came to know the decision of the Vicerory and the Mission. He complained of a breach of promise and asked the Viceroy to let the League form a government or to postpone the elections of the Constituent Assembly. As the two proposals of the Mission formed one whole, he argued it undesirable to proceed with the election of the Constituent Assembly and to postpone the formation of the Interim Government. He stated on June 28 : "I would like to emphasize that if any attempt is made to whittle down in any way the assurances given the Moslem League or to change or modify the basis of the statement of June 16 which has been accepted by the Moslem League, it will be regarded by Moslem India as going back on the part of the Cabinet Delegation and Vicerory on their pledged word in writing and as a breach of faith."[66]

But with all his sympathies for the League, Wavell had to abide the decision of the Mission and rejected Jinnah's argument. After this decision, the Cabinet Ministers left for England on June 29.[67]

65. S. I. N. C., II, pp. ccxxii-ccxxii.
66. *Voice of India*, Washington, September 1946, p. 333.
67. MBN, p. 313.

CHAPTER III

MUSLIM LEAGUE'S REACTION TO THE CABINET MISSON : DIRECT ACTION AND HINDU-MUSLIM RIOTS

The acceptance of Muslim League to join in the Interim Government, resulting in Mission's rulling of rejecting the offer, made Jinnah out of temper. His prospect of capturing central government had vanished. He was now no longer interested to join in the Constitution-making body, in the face of Congress's constant opposition of compulsory grouping of the Provinces. This opposition seemed unlikely to yield Pakistan within or without the Indian Union. The proposed Constituent Assembly seemed to him a trap. Through this body the Congress on the one hand, might destroy the idea of Pakistan and on the other, might create a strong central government for India.[1]

In the first week of July, Nehru stressed the need of the Constituent Assembly for India's independence. In a long speech delivered at All-India Congress Committee meeting, Nehru clarified the idea of independence, when "there must be no foreign domination in India." The Congress wanted to establish the republic of India. The Constituent Assembly which the Mission had advocated for India, was not that the Congress desired for; but it contained the seeds of India's "proper revolutionary Constituent Assembly". So the Congress was to take advantage of the present offer to use it for India's own advantage. Congress was to join in that Assembly so long it would suit the purpose of the country and might reject it, if it yield injury for the cause of India.[2]

Meanwhile Nehru's July 10 Conference had, at times, been regarded as 'explosive' that changed the course of history. Yet even before July 10, Nehru had explained his reservations about the Cabinet Mission's Plan. The League also made objections, at

1. Pandey, *Nehru*, p. 267.
2. V. I., p. 336.

the time, Mission's both long-range and short-range plans. Although the League originally had stated that it accepted the Mission's May 16 statement, but at the end of June, the League had announced its displeasure at "breaking the solemn pledges" by both the Cabinet Mission and the Viceroy, in connection with the Interim Government Plan. The League also suspected the willingness of the Congress to accept the Mission's long-range plan only "conditionally", which finally led them to criticise Nehru's July 10 remarks.

Under such a background the Congress thought that the League might not participate in the forthcoming Constituent Assembly, for lack of assurance that the fundamental principles of the Cabinet Mission's scheme would be adhered to. The League on the other hand believed that the Congress had only agreed to enter the Constituent Assembly in order to frame a Constitution according to its own wishes. While pointing to the need for a fresh statement of Britain's intentions, the League simultaneously blamed Congress. The League had also doubts about the advisability of entering into any fresh negotiations, the Viceroy might start for formation of an Interim Government. Moreover on July 9, when the League announced its Council to be convened in Bombay on July 28, and 29, the Congress anticipated some dangers from the League.[3]

In a press conference held at Bombay on July 10, Nehru made it clear that the Congress had made no commitment with regard to either the long-term or the short-term plan of the Cabinet Mission, except to enter the Constituent Assembly.[4] "The first thing is we have agreed to go into it and we have agreed to nothing else", stated Nehru. The Congress would inevitably go to the Constituent Assembly, where they were entirely and absolutely free in determining the issues. The Congress had not committed anything to anyone. "Naturally", Nehru continued, "even though one might not agree to commit oneself, there is a certain compulsion of facts which makes one accept this thing or that thing". Nehru further stated that according to Cabinet Mission, the Consti-

3. Indian Annual Register, Vol. II, July 10, 1964, p. 145.
4. From Press Conference, July 10, 1946.

tuent Assembly was more or less, a sovereign body, subjected to two considerations; the one was the proper arrangement for minorities, while another, a treaty between India and England. In regard to minorities, Nehru believed that the Congress might be able to solve it. About the treaty with Britain, Nehru remarked : "We shall have no treaty if they seek to impose anything on us". So Nehru proclaimed that "these two limiting factors to the sovereignty of the Constituent Assembly are not accepted by us".[5] Nehru also believed that the Constituent Assembly which was going to form shortly, bound to have conflicts with the Caretaker Government. The Caretaker Government had neither any stability nor any possibility of its long continuance.

Nehru was also in favour of a strong central government. Though the Cabinet Mission had proposed only four basic subjects, Defence, Foreign Affairs, Communications and the powers to raise finances for these, within the purview of the centre, still there were enough scope to increase their activities. Defence and communications had large industries behind them; while the External Affairs inevitably was to include foreign trade policy. Referring to the question of raising finances for the Union, Nehru commented that the "Central Government must raise its finances by taxation." Nehru was in favour of a strong central government and also it was to work as a co-ordinating body among the Provinces. "There must be some over-all power to intervene in grave crises, breakdown of the administration or economic breakdown or famine. The scope of the Centre, even though limited, inevitably grows, because it cannot exist otherwise,"[6] remarked Nehru in the Press Conference at Bombay. This declaration of Nehru led many people to believe that in the Provisional Government, the Congress was to interprete everything according to its own will.

Maulana Azad reacted sharply on Nehru's Press Conference on July 10. According to him, the Press Conference was "one of those unfortunate events which changed the course of history."[7]

5. Dorothy. *Nehru*, II, p. 237.
6. I. A. R., II, July 10, 1946, pp. 145-147.
7. Azad stated that "this was one of the greatest tragedies of Indian history and I have to say with the deepest of regret that a large part of the responsibility for this development rests with Jawaharlal."—Azad, I. W. F., p. 170.

After the above Conference, Azad himself addressed Nehru : "You have changed the entire basis of the agreement with England." Azad was perturbed by Nehru's remark of July 10, himself stated on the same date : "If unfortunately, any insuperable difficulties crop up in direct conflict with our fundamental principles, we shall not hesitate to kill the Constituent Assembly."[8]

In the month of July, it appeared that an Interim Government might finally come into existence. Nehru continued to argue in favour of an independent Constituent Assembly which was to work against communal hatred, for protection of minorities and a United democratic India. The high tension created constant difficulties among Nehru, Jinnah and Wavell. Distrust existed on all sides. On the question of grouping, Nehru pointed out that it was highly likely that North-West Frontier Province and Assam would decide against grouping, in which case sections B and C would certainly collapse. Thus Nehru made numerous observations in conjunction with proposals put forward by the Cabinet Mission. The Legislative assembly of Assam then passed a resolution at the instance of the Congress Premier Gopinath Bardoloi boycotting section C in which the province was placed.[9]

The speeches of Nehru were not inconsistent with the Congress interpretation of May 16 proposal, but they placed Jinnah

8. I. A. R., II, July 10, 1946, p. 144.

At a later Press Conference, in reply to question about Azad's criticism, Nehru said : "I am sorry to confess that I have no very clear ideas of the day occurrences in those days; it was a great burden on all of us—a burden of decision.....Whether that was a right analysis or a wrong analysis, I cannot say. I am only saying that it had a powerful effect on our thinking. And, even in the course of the Interim Government, we had proposed the appointment of a Planning Commission. It had been opposed by the Moslem League representatives. So that, in every such matter where economic considerations and planning came in, we were likely to come up against inner pulls in different directions.... So, how can I judge how far I am responsible ? Mine was certainly part of the responsibility, and Maulana Azad Sahib may be completely right in thinking that I acted wrongly".—Azad, I. W. F., as quoted in introduction by Lious Fischer, pp. xxii-xxiv.

9. Nehru to Bardoloi, July 22. All-India Congress Committee Papers, File No. 71, 1946-47.

in an embarrassing position in relation to his followers. These speeches of Nehru publicly destroyed the very prospect of Pakistan, claimed sovereign rights for the Constituent Assembly and scraped the compulsory grouping of the provinces. Moreover the outcome of the Constituent Assembly elections went in favour of the Congress, where out of 296 seats, the Congress secured 209.[10] This naturally made Jinnah disturbed. Over and above this, during his negotiations with Jinnah, Nehru still insisted on Congress's right to include a non-League Muslim in its quota for the Interim Government. The Congress also advocated that as the League had withdrawn its acceptance of May 16 proposal, the latter was no longer qualified to be included in the government. Thus on July 29, the Muslim League, after making due references to Nehru's speeches, withdrew its acceptance of the Cabinet Mission Plan.[11] Also to meet the end of justice in its own way, the Muslim League passed its July 29 Resolution calling for 'Direct Action', which meant violence against the non-Muslims.

Just a week before the League passed its Resolution, the Viceroy resumed its efforts to convince both Nehru and Jinnah that a coalition Interim Government at the Centre might be formed, giving assurances that Britain would consider the new government as a Dominion Government. Britain would also recognise "the greatest possible freedom" to the new government in the exercise of its day-to-day administration. He also agreed that the Congress was now free to nominate one or more nationalist Muslims to the Interim Government. But Nehru declined the offer this time also, on the ground that the Congress attached great importance to what it termed "independence in action" on the part of the new government. Since the status and power of a Provisional Interim Government must be decided in unambiguous language, Nehru concluded that he was wholly unable to co-operate on the formation of a Government on the terms suggested by Wavell.[12]

The formation of the Constituent Assembly greatly disturbed Jinnah. He demanded the postponement of the Assembly as the Constituent Assembly and the Interim Government hung together.

10. Muller, I. W. I., p. 154,
11. Pandey, *Nehru*, p. 268.
12. Pyarelal, *Mahatma Gandhi*, Vol. I, p. 264,

But the Viceroy denied this assertion and refused to postpone the Assembly. Jinnah's immediate reaction was the League's refusal to participate in the short-range as well as the long-range arrangements. Thus on the very day of July 29, the League resolved to resort to direct action to achieve Pakistan. Preceding to the 'direct action', the League made mainly the following resolutions at its meeting held in Bombay on July 27 :

"The scheme of the Cabinet Delegation fell far short of the demand of the Muslim Nation for the immediate establishment of an independent and fully sovereign state of Pakistan...with a view to ending the Hindu-Muslim deadlock peacefully.

"In arriving at this decision, the Council was also greatly influenced by the statement of the President, which he made with the authority of the Viceroy, that the Interim Government, which was an integral part of the Mission's scheme, was going to be formed on the basis of a formula, namely, five Muslim League, five Congress, one sikh and one Indian Christian or Anglo-Indian and the most important portfolios to be distributed equally between the two major parties, the Muslim League and the Congress.

"That the British Government have committed a breach of faith with the Muslim League in that the Cabinet Mission and the Viceroy went back on the original formula of 5 : 5 : 2 for the setting up of the Interim Government to placate the Congress.

"Accordingly, on June 16, the President of the Muslim League received a Statement embodying what was announced to be the final decision for setting up the Interim Government by the Viceroy, making it clear that if either of the two major parties refused to accept the statement of June 16, the Viceroy would proceed to form the Interim Government with the major party accepting it and such other representatives as were willing to join.

"Even this final decision of the Cabinet Mission of the 16th June with regard to the formation of the Interim Government was rejected by the Congress, whereas the Muslim League definitely accepted it—although it was different from the original formula....

"The Viceroy, however, scrapped the proposal of June 16 and postponed the formation of the Interim Government on the plea concocted by the legalistic talents of the Cabinet Mission...to the effect that as both the major parties...had accepted the statement of May 16, the question of Interim Government could only be taken up in consultation with the representatives of both the parties.

"The result is that of the two major parties, the Muslim League alone has accepted the statements of May 16 and 25 according to the spirit and letter of the proposals embodied therein. Inspite of the attention of the Secretary of State for India having been drawn to this situation by the statement of the President of the Muslim League on July 13...neither Sir Stafford Cripps in the House of Commons nor Lord Pethick Lawrence in the House of Lords, have provided or suggested any means or machinery to prevent the Constituent Assembly from taking decisions which would be ultra vires and not competent for the Assembly to do so

"Once the Constituent Assembly has been summoned and met, there is no provision or power that could prevent any decision from being taken by the Congress with its overwhelming majority. .... It would rest entirely with the majority to take such decisions as they may think proper to suit them; the Congress has already secured by sheer number an overwhelming Hindu caste majority and they will be in a position to use the Assembly in the manner in which they have already declared....

"The attitude of Congress clearly shows that these conditions precedent for the successful working of the Constitution—making body do not exist. This fact, taken together with the Policy of the British Government of sacrificing the interests of the Muslim nation,...to appease the Congress and the way in which they have been going back on their...assurances given from time to time to the Muslims, leave no doubt that in these circumstances the participation of the Muslims in the proposed constitution-making machinery is fraught with danger and the Council, therefore, hereby withdraws its acceptance of the Cabinet Mission's proposals.'[13]

13. Resolutons of the All-India Muslim League, July 27, (*vide*, S. I. N. C., II, pp. ccxxvii-ccxxix).

Two days after, on July 29, the League called for "Direct Action" and set up a Council of Action, reminding the Muslims that "it was in the month of *Ramzan* that the first open conflict Between Islam and Heathenism was fought and won by three hundred and thirteen Muslims in Arabia." The League declared crusade announcing that ten crores of Indian Muslims who through bad luck had become slaves of Hindus and the British.[14] Thus the League declared *Jehad*, and the whole country was actually on the verge of a civil war.

The Muslim League also made the following resolution on "Direct Action" :

"Whereas the All-India Muslim League has to-day resolved to reject the proposals embodied in the statement of the Cabinet Mission and the Viceroy dated May 16, 1946, due to the intransigence of the Congress on one hand, and the breach of faith with the Muslims by the British Government, on the other, and whereas Muslim India has exhausted, without success, all efforts to find a peaceful solution of the Indian problem by compromise and constitutional means; and whereas the Congress is bent upon setting up a Caste Hindu Raj in India with the connivance of the British; and whereas recent events have shown that power politics and not justice and fairplay are the deciding factors in Indian affairs; and whereas it has become abundantly clear that the Muslims of India would not rest content with anything less than the immediate establishment of an independent and full sovereign state of Pakistan and would resist any attempt to impose any Constitution, long-term or short-term, or setting up of any Interim Government at the Centre without the approval or consent of the Muslim League, the Council of the All-India Muslim League is convinced that now the time has come for the Muslims nation to resort to direct action to achieve Pakistan and assert their just rights and to vindicate their honour and to get rid of the present slavery under the British and contemplated future caste Hindu domination.

"This Council calls upon the Muslim nation to stand to a man behind their sole representative organisation, the All-India Muslim League, and be ready for every sacrifice. This Council

14. Pyarelal, *Mahatma Gandhi*, Vol. I, pp. 251-253.

directs the Working Committee to prepare forthwith a programme of direct action to carry out the policy initiated above and to organise the Muslims for the coming struggle to be launched as and when necessary. As a protest against and in token of their deep resentment of the attitude of the British, this Council calls upon the Muslims to renounce forthwith the titles conferred upon them by the alien Government."[15]

The Muslim League, as a part of their direct action programme, began to circulate a leaflet bearing the picture of Jinnah with sword in his hand, stated: "We Muslims have had the Crown and have ruled. Be ready and take your swords. O. Kafer ! .... your doom is not far and the general massacre will come !" In conjunction with the plans for August 16, Jinnah announced: "Today we bid good-bye to Constitutional method." He again exclaimed: "We have...forged a pistol and are in a position to use it."[16]

Muslim League authorised Jinnah to take any action he liked for the programme of direct action. It was then not clear to Jinnah himself and the Leaguers generally thought that there would be another meeting of the Muslim League Council to work out in details about their future plan.[17] But his followers were not totally in dark about the programme. Liaqat Ali Khan—the Secretary of the League believed that they could resort to any unconstitutional action as they were not the followers of non-violence. Khawaja Najmuddin, the leader of the Muslim League in Bengal propagated for any action beneficial for the Muslims. Abdur Rab Nishtar went one step further and declared their goal to achieve Pakistan only through bloodshed.[18]

The declaration of Direct Action immediately led to communal fanaticism resulting in murder and assassination in different parts of India. Before 'the Great Calcutta-Killings' on August 16, reports began to come from Ahmedabad, Bombay, Allahabad,

15. Quoted in S. I. N. C., II, P. ccxxix.
16. Pyarelal, *Mahatma Gandhi*, I, pp. 251-253.
17. Azad, I. W. F., p. 168. When an India press-reporter asked Jinnah what did he mean by "direct action", the latter replied that he was not prepared at present to disclose it.—Pyarelal, *Mahatma Gandhi*, Vol. I, p. 240.
18. Pyarelal, *Mahatma Gandhi*, Vol. I, pp. 240-241.

Aligarh, Dacca and some other places about the killing of the innocent people.[19] It created tense situation in different parts of India as the League's Direct Action seemed to be of different type. The people of Calcutta believed that the League might attack the Congressmen and loot their property. The panic became further accelerated when the Bengal Government decided to declare August 16, a public holiday. It created a general sense of insecurity in Calcutta due to the fact that the Bengal Government was under the control of the Muslim League headed by H. S. Suhrawardy as the Prime Minister.[20]

Some historians had advanced arguments that neither the Congress nor the League had ever truely accepted the Cabinet Mission Plan, despite having at one time or another formally approved it and no one had as yet found an acceptable method of doing so.[21] And as the Viceroy had no other plan to advance, the Direct Action resolution of the Muslim League as well as their withdrawal from the Cabinet Mission Plan accomplished what Congress had failed so far to do. A reaction of the British Cabinet was reported to Gandhiji from London by one of his friends: "After Jinnah's threat (of Direct Action), the British Cabinet asked the Viceroy to send for Jinnah and tell (him) that if he was not prepared to play the game, the British Cabinet had decided to hand over responsibility to the Congress and such other people as were prepared to work with them and to go ahead without Jinnah."[22]

The British Government in Britain and India realised a good shaking the League was 'badly needed' for Jinnah's outburst. So, on August 6, 1946, the Viceroy, acting under the direction from London, invited Nehru to submit proposals for formation of an Interim Government.[23]

The communal tension created by Jinnah's declaration on the one hand, and Viceroy's appeal to form the Interim Government

19. Bandyopadhyaya, Sailesh Kumar, *Jinna : Pakistan, Natun Bhabna* (Calcutta, New Edn., 1996 B. S.), p. 241.
20. Azad, I. W. F., pp. 168-169. The Congress party in Bengal Assembly protested against the declaration of a public holiday, but this proved ineffective.
21. MBN, p. 317.
22. Quoted in Dorothy, *Nehru*, II, p. 243.
23. *Ibid.*

on the other, created a tense atmosphere for the Congress. Accordingly the Congress tried to create a congenial atmosphere in the country by reviewing the whole situation. So the Working Committee of the Congress met on August 8, where Azad pointed out that the Congress should adopt a resolution making it clear "that the statement of the Congress President at the Bombay Press Conference was his personal opinion and did not conform the decision of the Congress." This decision of Azad placed Nehru in a very awkward position. In the words of Azad which had been released thirty years after his death[24], he observed : "Jawaharlal argued that he had no objection if the Working Committee wanted to reiterate that the Cabinet Mission Plan has been accepted by the Congress, but felt that it would be embarrassing to the organisation and also to him personally if the Working Committee passed a resolution that the statement of the Congress President did not represent the policy of the Congress."

The Congress Working Committee now involved in a dilemma on the one side, and the prestige of the Congress President on the other. "To repudiate the President's statement would weaken the organisation", remarked Azad, "but to give up the Cabinet Mission Plan would ruin the country". So the Congress finally drafted a resolution making no reference to Nehru's statement, reaffirmed the decision of the Congress : "The Working Committee regret to note that the Council of the All India Muslim League, reversing their previous decision, have decided not to participate in the Constituent Assembly. In this period of rapid transition from dependence on a foreign power to full independence, when vast and intricate political and economic problems have to be faced and solved, the largest measure of co-operation among the people of India and their representatives is called for, so that the change-over should be smooth and to the advantage of all concerned. The Committee realise that there are differences in the outlook and objectives of the Congress and the Muslim

---

24. The Calcutta High Court, the Delhi High Court and the Supreme Court, before the Justice B. N. Kirpal of the Delhi High Court directed on September 29, 1988, that a copy of the text deposited in the National Library, Calcutta, and in the National Archives, New Delhi, be published.—Publisher's note on Azad, I. W. F.

League. Nevertheless, in the larger interests of the country as a whole and of the freedom of the people of India, the Committee appeal for the co-operation of all those who seek the freedom and good of the country, in the hope that cooperation in common tasks may lead to the solution of many of India's problems... It was with this object and with the desire to function in the Constituent Assembly and make it a success, that the Working Committee passed their resolution on June 26, 1946 which was subsequently ratified by the All India Congress Committee on July 7, 1946... The Committee hope that the Muslim League and all others concerned, in their winder interests of the nation as well as of their own, will join in this great task".[25]

Congress hoped that this resolution would save the situation as because now the "Congress had accepted the Cabinet Mission Plan in its entirety". But Jinnha did not accept the Congress statement true and held that Nehru's Press Conference at Bombay represented "the real mind of the Congress". He advanced his arguments that If the Congress could change its resolutions so many times before the British left India; there was no guarantee after British left India, that the Congress would not go back to its former views reflected by Nehru's earlier statement.[26] So Jinnha and the Muslim League remained adamant to carry on their declared principle of Direct Action.

When the tension was rapidly drifting to a communal-riot and no stable interim government could have been formed to check such an atmosphere surcharged with suspicion and hatred, Nehru again took the initiative on the advise of Wavell to form a government at the centre with the help of Jinnah. Nehru approached Jinnah several times for conciliation and compromise, but the latter became bitterly critical[27] of what he described as 'the caste Hindu Fascist Congress' who tried 'to dominate and rule over the Musalmans and other minority communities of India with the aid of British bayonets'.[28] Thus on August 16, the 'Direct

25. Quoted in Azad, I. W. F., pp. 166-167.
26. *Ibid.*, p. 167.
27. Moon, *Gandhi*, p. 248.
28. Nanda, B. R., *Mahatma Gandhi—A Biography* (London, 1958), pp. 491-492.

Action Day' was celebrated by the Muslim League which shook the whole country, by a series of reaction of violent explosions, in the succeeding one year.

The 'Great Calcutta Killing' started on August 16, in the morning of 7 A. M. from Maniktola area. Indiscriminate murder of the Hindus including men, women, children took place suddenly for which the Hindus were totally unprepared. Arson, loot and outraging the chastity of women became the common feature. It is said that over 5000 lives were lost between August 16 to August 20, in Calcutta, basides the wounded numbered 15,000.[29] Processions were taken out by the League on the Calcutta streets who started to loot and committed acts of arson which destroyed the property of crores of rupees. Soon the whole city was in the grip of the *goondas*. Sarat Chandra Bose immediately met the Governor and asked him to bring the sitution under control but the Governor did not take any action, as he was definite that the riot was not anti-British.[30] Maulana Azad, on his way to Delhi came to Dum Dum airport. On the way, he saw the military standing inactively. When asked they replied to Azad that their duty "were not helping in restoring order", but "were to stand ready and not to take any action".[31] The Calcutta police and military remained as silent spectators, while innocent people were brutally murdered.

Suhrawardy, the Primer as well as the leader of the Muslim League in Bengal, could not escape responsibility of the Great Calcutta Killing. Charges were levelled against the Provincial Government that Suhrawardy deliberately prevented the police to take prompt action when riot broke out in Calcutta.[32] But Jinnah declared it as a systematic Hindu conspiracy to discredit the League Ministry in Bengal. He led the whole responsibility to

---

29. Bandyopadhyay, *Jinnah*, p. 242.
30 *Ibid.*, pp. 242-242. "Mr. Jinnah had called the Direct Action Day's demonstration against the British for their refusal to recognize Pakistan but of all the communities in Calcutta once the rioting began, the British were the only ones who were safe".—Mosley, Leonard, *The Last Days of the British Raj* (London, 1961), p. 31.
31. Azad, I. W. F., p. 169.
32. NMG, p. 493.

Cabinet Mission, Congress and on Gandhiji.[33] Some Muslim leaders also levelled charges against Hindu Mahasabha for such a situation and they chose Calcutta because "Bengal was the only province in India which had a Muslim League ministry".[34]

But on the third day when Hindus and Sikhs organised themselves and jumped on the Muslims for taking revenge, Suhrawardy came to his senses. "It was only when the Hindus and Sikhs had come out in retaliation that the Chief Minister (Suhrawardy) had called for military aid".[35] Now the Hindus took the upper-hand for their numerical superiority in Calcutta and hit back savagely.[36] Thus Suhrawardy could not sit idle for the murder of thousands of Muslims in Calcutta and personally directed the police to stop this madness. He went to the Police Control office at Lalbazar and gave them necessary directions.[37] For this act, Suhrawardy was publicly criticised by the press, not to take proper action in time.

Within two months, the Calcutta-Killing soon had repurcussions in the Muslim majority district of Noakhali in East Bengal, where encouraged by fanatic priests and politicians, the local people began to burn the property of the Hindus and desecrating their temples. They adopted various ways of atrocities like the forcible conversion of the Hindus and outraging the chastity of Hindu women.[38] Thousands of Hindus, fled in terror, to West Bengal and Bihar. Such inhumanities had no parallel in the history of mankind that had been practised in the name of religion for gaining political ends.

Gandhiji was deeply shocked when the news of the communal riots in East Bengal reached him. He was particularly hurt by the crimes against women. "All his life he had believed in non-

33. Pyarelal, *Mahatma Gandhi*, Vo.. I, p. 245.
34. Ahmad, Kamruddin, *The Social History of East Pakistan* (Dacca, 2nd Edn., 1967), p. 78.
35. Mosley, *The British Raj*, p. 33.
36. The impression went abroad that inspite of a Muslim League ministry in Bengal, the Hindus had won in this trial of strength in Calcutta.
37. Kamruddin, *East Pakistan*, p. 78.
38. NMG, p. 494.

violence and Hindu-Muslim unity", remarked his biographer, Penderel Moon, "but now, on the threshold of independence, Hindus and Muslims were at each other's throats".[39] *Swaraj* that was coming seemed far from the *swaraj* of his dreams. He decided therefore to leave for East Bengal cancelling all his programmes in Delhi. Friends tried to stop his journey as his health was poor and he reached the old age of 77. But now by his natural instinct, he was gradually drifting away from power and devoted himself to the direct service of the people. He became politically ineffectual but the remaining months of his life were morally the crown of his career. A saint had now come forward from politician.

When Gandhiji reached Calcutta, he saw the savages of the August riots. He met with a number of people including the British Governor and the Primier Suhrawardy. Meanwhile the news of the murder of the Hindus of Noakhali inflamed Bihar, where retaliation and murder of the Muslims surcharged the whole atmosphere with panic. Hindus of Bihar described this riot as the "revenge of Noakhali" and the Muslims began to be murdered at Patna, Mungher, Bhagalpur, Santhal Parganas and many places in the province.[40] The Congress government of Bihar seemed unable to control the situation. But it was Nehru, then the head of the Interim Government, who flew to Patna, and "threatened to resort to aerial hombing to quell the disturbances".[41] So the Bihar riots had been subsided by intervention of Nehru.

But riots continued unabated in Noakhali and so Gandhiji decided, on October 27, to go there personally. He devoted himself wholeheartedly to his mission in Noakhali and suspended all other activities. At Noakhali, he prepared every day a lesson in Bengali, receiving visitors, holding prayer meetings and preaching to the people on fearlessnass and forgiveness. In East Bengal Gandhiji began his journey from one village to another. He settled down for several weeks in the village of Srirampur in Noakhali district, where he found that out of 200 Hindu families only three had remained after the recent riots. From Srirampur,

39. Moon, *Gandhi*, p. 249.
40. Bandyopadhyay, *Jinnah*, p. 251.
41. Moon, *Gandhi*, p. 250

he dispersed his companions to settle in different villages;[42] While Gandhiji himself remained there with Manu Gandhi, his stenographer Parsuram and his Bengali interpretor Prof. Nirmal Kumar Bose, his own ambition was 'to wipe every tear from every eye'.

But the restoration of confidence between the two communities was a difficult task. Soon the Muslims discovered in Gandhiji "a deep political game". Even the Bengal Primier Suhrawardy, who at first welcomed him, became critical of his long stay in East Bengal. Muslims began to ask him why he did not undertake tour in Bihar to relieve the Muslims from the hands of the Hindus. Nehru had been urging him repeatedly to return to Delhi. But these could not deflect him from his journey. Walking barefoot, he covered a distance of 116 miles visiting 47 villages. But these criticism hurt him and he recorded in his diary on January 2, 1947 : "God's grace alone is sustaining me. I can see there is some grave defects in me somewhere which is the cause of all this. All round me is utter darkness. When will God take me out of the darkness into his Light ?"[43] Now Gandhiji did not want to live for 125 years as he professed earlier.

Gandhiji remained in Bengal from October 1946 to the end of February 1947. In the beginning of March, he came to Bihar and advised the majority to repent, while the minority must forgive. He collected subscriptions from Hindus for the relief of the Muslim sufferers and directed the Bihar Government for the re-settlement of the Muslims.[44] Thus while the condition of Bihar was gradually improved, news reached in every corner of India about the outbreak of communal riots in Bombay and the Punjab. Anti-Pakistan demonstrations were held in Lahore on March 4, resulting in the death of 13 persons while injury to many. Communal disturbances soon spread to Amritsar and Rawalpindi.[45]

The news of the Punjab disturbances reached Gandhiji when he was in Bihar. The Hindu and Sikh minorities in West Punjab had experienced the same horrors suffered by the Hindu minority

42. Kanu Gandhi, Sucheta Kripalani, Sushila, Abha and Pyarelal, each of them were directed to settle in a village.
43. Quoted in Moon, *Gandhi*, p. 252.
44. NMG, p. 497.
45. Azad, I. W. F., p. 196.

in East Bengal. The order was at last restored by the help of military, but tension continued in the Punjab. Gandhiji was much bewildered. Since October 1946, he had been wandering from one Province after another in a vain attempt to curb violence. While his work was settled in one province, there was an outbreak in another. These communal disturbances shocked Gandhiji greatly. He began to blame himself and could not help feeling "a deep sense of failure."[46]

Nehru had a great reaction on riots. He had deep sympathy for the victims of both communities. While India's independence was so near, the riots struck him as a blow to his hopes of a free India. "There appears to be a competition in murder and brutality," he said in course of moving reports to the Central Assembly.[47] On August 26, 1946, just before the formation of the Interim Government, Nehru suggested how to fight the gangsters by observing : "Calcutta has been a terrible lesson.... The new development of violence, involving stabbing, arson and looting, chiefly in cities, obviously cannot be tolerated or else all organised life would become impossible." According to him, it had become a challenge to 'every decent instinct of humanity'. He reminded the people "that during the past twenty-six years of repeated conflict on an intensive and mass scale between the nationalist movement and the British power in India, nothing of this kind has happended." Every citizen had his own responsibility and in such a crisis" it is an obligation of every citizen to discharge his responsibility."[48]

Nehru also made a broadcast to the nation on violence in the Punjab. As he was the believer of non-violence, he observed in his speech : "What is happening now is something directly inimical, and so directly opposed to these ideals. The very thought of it shames me, and makes me sometimes doubt if all the good work that we have done in these many years is not going to bear fruit at all. And yet that doubt cannot remain for long. For I do believe that good work must bear good results just as I do

46. NMG, p. 500.
47. MBN, p. 321.
48. Bright, J. S., *Important Speeches of Jawaharlal Nehru 1922-1946* Vol. I (Lahore, 3rd Edn.), p. 390.

believe that evil must bear evil consequences. There has been enough of evil work in this country. Let us put an end to it, and start good work, and try to follow the great lessons that the Mahatma has taught us."[49]

For the outbreak of communal riots, Nehru became very restive, but so long he could not visit Bengal and Bihar due to the formation of the Interim Government through which he aspired the freedom of India. Earlier he wrote several letters to Wavell to bring the situation under control, but bore no fruits. He began to receive daily telegrams from East Bengal and sometimes from Calcutta, giving in details about the stabbing, murder and looting in East Bengal.[50] Thus Nehru wanted that the Viceroy would do something for relieving the people from distress, but the latter only appreciated the anxiety of Nehru. So Nehru again wrote Wavell on October 15, 1946 about the cruelities perpetrated in East Bengal and instead of being stopped in time, it was allowed to grow. He then led the whole blame on Bengal Government by observing : "Bengal, which has long led India in many ways, has rapidly become a shambles and a ruin. It is a small matter to discuss legal responsibilities when such a horrible catastrophe overtakes a people. It is evident that the Bengal Government is completely incapable of controlling the situation. Indeed, many people think that they have no desire to control it." Nehru became greatly perturbed and felt that either "we must face this issue somehow or we retire from the public scene."[51]

On October 31, a meeting of some prominent citizens of Calcutta under the chairmanship of Sarat Chandra Bose called for a general strike from November 4 to 13, in protest against the failure of the League Government to prevent lawlessness in Bengal since August 16. In view of such a possibility of general strike in Calcutta, Nehru and Patel felt that they should visit Calcutta with-

49. MJS, p. 343.
50. Haran Chandra Ghosh Choudhury, President, Noakhali District Congress Committee informed Nehru about the murder and loot in his district, including the murder of the President of local Bar Association.
51. Nehru's letter to Wavell, October 15, 1946 (Quoted in S. Gopal (Edt.), *Selected Works of Jawaharlal Nehru*, Second Series, Vol. I, New Delhi, 1984, pp. 51-52).

out any loss of time and accordingly reached at Dum Dum airport on November 2, with two other League leaders—Nishtar and Liaqat Ali. This ghastly acts in Bengal, Nehru felt was "sufficient to wake up the dead." On Suhrawardy's suggestion, Nehru issued a joint appeal[52] to the people of Calcutta to cease violence by observing : "We venture to make an urgent and earnest appeal to all of our countrymen, not only in Calcutta and Bengal but all over India. Much has happened in the recent past which has degraded Indian humanity and shamed us before others. Whatever our differences might be, none of us should tolerate acts which degrade and brutalise our people. That ignoble method brings no solution, and on that basis we can build no edifice of freedom. Violence against a neighbour and fellow citizen leads to counter and increasing violence and to the drying up of social and civil life. It leads to human degradation. We plead therefore most earnestly for a cessation of this violence and for a return to the methods of peace."[53] He also visited some relief centres in Calcutta.

After making his appeal to the people of Bengal, Nehru made a hurricane tour in different parts of Bihar and arrived in Patna in the evening of November 3. On November 4, he addressed the people of Fatwa, Khusrupore, Bakhtiarpur, Harnaut, Biharsharif and Patna appealing to their senses : "The *goonda* who sets fire to the house of his neighbour, who kills his friends is public enemy no. I. He must be eliminated and all efforts must be concentrated to that end." At Patna he appealed to the people to realise that India had reached the door of freedom but "we are doing something that will block our onward march."[54] Nehru then went to Munghyr on November 5 and addressed a public meeting by observing : "Unless the people of Bihar make active and sincere efforts even now to quench the fire of communalism and violence it would lead to huge conflagation fanned by ill will, hatred and distrust and would burn to ashes every one of them in

52. The joint appeal was issued by Nehru, Liaqat Ali, Patel and Nishtar, at Calcutta on November 3, 1946.
53. GSW, p. 54.
54. The Searchlight, November 6, 1946.
55. Speech at Munghyr, The Searchlight, November 9.

the end along with all that had been achieved by the sacrifices of so many of their countrymen."[55] So he advised them to be ashamed of their acts and urged them to restore peace in the province.

On October 25, a Noakhali Day was observed in various parts of Bihar. A huge procession was taken out in Patna and a very big meeting was held. It was followed by the trouble at Chhapra on October 26 and also in rural areas. Soon Bhagalpur also caught fire. On October 31, the people of Patna attacked Muslim houses and burnt them down, killed many Muslims and looted their property. It was due to the timely intervention of Nehru and some prominent leaders of Bihar[56] the situation brought back to normalcy to a great extent, though undercurrent suspicions continued.

Nehru returned to Delhi on November 9[57], leaving Rajendra Prasad and Jayaprakash Narayan in Patna for restoring peace between the two communities. He became satisfied that the situation in Bihar had been much improved "and no major development is expected in future". He believed that the report of the Muslims killing in Bihar had been much "exaggerated", which had no relation to fact. "It is very difficult to access the exact number of people killed, wounded and stranded", observed Nehru in an interview to the Associated Press of America in Patna, "but it can never be probably over 2,000 killed at the utmost on all counts, including military firing".[58]

Before his arrival in Delhi, Nehru prepared a note on November 6, narrating the causes of disturbacces in Bihar. He attributed them largely to the Muslim League and the Hindu Mahasabha, by observing : "Since the Muslim League adopted Pakistan as its objective and started even before that an agitation

56. Some of the Congress leaders in Bihar like Prabhunath Singh Girish Tiwari, Dwarka Nath Tiwari and some others tried bravely to control the situation in Saran district. The efforts of Jagat Narayan Lal, Singheswar Prasad and some others bore fruit in Patna.
57. Nehru returned to Delhi by air in view of certain communal troubles in Meerut.
58. Nehru's interview in Patna, November 9 (*Vide, The Hindu*, November 10, 1946).

based on hatred and bitter denunciation of the Congress as well as of the Hindus generally, reactions gradually began to set in which were taken advantage of by the Hindu Mahasabha and like organizations. This did not affect the widespread popularity of the Congress among the Hindu masses so far as the political issues were concerned But it did produce communal feeling and a tendency among the middle class to criticize the Congress for not supporting the Hindu cause as against the Muslim League". In the same note, he narrated about the causes of retaliation in Hindu mind : "One notice, purporting to be issued on behalf of the Muslim League, was widely circulated in many parts of India and especially in Bihar. This gave instructions to kill Hindus, loot their property and do various other highly objectionable things in order to establish Pakistan... They (the people of Bihar) became utterly convinced that the Muslim League was bent on indulging in the most heinous crime in pursuance of its policy of direct action. This, they thought, had to be resisted at any cost".[59]

In a long statement issued on December 1, 1946, the Bihar Muslim League demanded "the exchange of population since it would be impossible for the Muslim minority here to live under perpetual fear and dread of mob violence". This gave rise to panic in East Bangal and created high tensions in the mind of the Hindu minority. During this time, Nehru came to Noakhali, his mission was to stand against communalism as well as to seek advice from Gandhiji "in regard to many matters". While he was addressing a crowd at Chaumuhani on December 27 at night, on his way to Srirampur in Noakhali district, where Gandhiji was preaching his theory of non-violence, Nehru was hit by a brick hurled by an unknown person.[60] When he met Gandhiji at Srirampur, the latter showed him the resolution of Bihar Provincial Muslim League, about which Nehru was in dark till then. On receiving this report, Nehru thought it necessary to apprise the Bihar situation and his role in Bihar, to Suhrawardy—the Primer of Bengal. From Srirampur, he wrote a letter to the Primier : "During this period I was intensively occupied in touring, visiting

59. Nehru's note written at the Circuit House, Patna, November 6, (*Vide*, J. N. Papers, Nehru Memorial Museum and Library).
60. GSW, p. 102.

numerous places in the affected areas, addressing large gatherings, and in Conferences with the ministers, officials, the military and Muslim League members. After five days it appeared to me that the trouble had ended or had been controlled". About the atrocities on the Muslims in Bihar, he further wrote : "There is no doubt that the most cruel and brutal murders on a large scale took place in Bihar", but "I found that very often they were greatly exaggerated and sometimes quite baseless".[61] He returned to Calcutta on December 30 and when asked by the Press-reporters about the situation in Noakhali, Nehru replied that "the life is not safe anywhere". He advised the Hindu refugees to go back to their villages as the situation had been gradually becoming normal.[62]

On his way to Delhi from Calcutta, Nehru halted at Patna, where he found the situation had been much improved from his previous visit. "Yet the Muslim League volunteers went about asking and influencing people to leave their homes and generally creating a psychology of fear", remarked Nehru sarcastically in his letter to Suhrawardy, observing further that "This has been done and is being done on a fairly widespread and organised basis".[63]

On the other hand, Jinnah did not believe in force but "believed in threats of force". After the 'Great Calcutta-Killing' and the consequence disturbances in Bihar and Bengal, communal violence became the strongest argument that guided Jinnah for creating Pakistan. He warned the Congress leaders that if India was not divided,[64] worse things would happen in future.

61. Nehru's letter to Suhrawardy. December 29, 1946 (quoted from GSW, pp. 97-91).
62. Nehru's Press interview in Calcutta December 30, 1946 (*The Hindu*, January 1, 1947).
63. Nehru's letter to Suhrawardy, January 1, 1947 (GSW, pp. 103-105.
64. NMG, p. 502.

CHAPTER IV

NEHRU-JINNAH TANGLE AND THE FORMATION OF THE INTERIM GOVERNMENT

Wavell had already invited Nehru on August 6, under the instructions from London for the formation of the Interim-Government at the Centre and if possible, with the help of the Muslim League. The Congress was now prepared to form the government and even modified Nehru's 10th July statement to appease Jinnah, but the latter remained adamant in his attitude. While welcoming Viceroy's invitation, Nehru wrote to him that any premature attempt to induce the League to join in the government might produce a contrary result. Such an attempt might bring communal controversy resulting further delay in forming the government. Nehru therefore suggested that the best course would be "to make a public announcement to the effect that he had invited the President of...Congress to form a Provisional Government and that the latter had accepted his invitation." After this announcement by the Viceroy, Nehru believed that it would be possible to invite the Muslim League to co-operate. Nehru even went one step further stating that in case of non-cooperation by the League, the Congress was alone prepared to go ahead without the consent of the League.[1]

The Congress Working Committee which met at Wardha closed with the offer and the Viceroy immediately announced on August 12, Congress President's acceptance of the invitation. After the anuouncement Nehru made another attempt to woo Jinnah. Accordingly the Congress passed another resolution addressing the League in sweet language, desiring its co-operation. Nehru himself promptly addressed Jinnah as he should co-operate in a business like manner. But Jinnah's reaction to this resolution was not unexpected. He made *volta face,* saw nothing new in

1. Pyarelal, *Mahatma Gandhi*, Vol. I, pp. 264-265,

it "but only old lamps under a new dome."[2] His only intention was then Direct Action.

Wavell regretted his action immediately after he extended invitation to Nehru to form the government. He even tried to recall his letter, but it was then too late. Thereafter, he tried utmost to bring the Leaguo into the Interim Government at any cost. Before he received the list of names of Nehru's government, Wavell repeatedly persuaded Jinnah to come into the Government.[3] Remarking on this persuation of Wavell, Nehru wrote to him that he had already accepted the offer on the understanding that it would be the responsibility of the Congress. Accordingly "I approached...Jinnah and sought the co-operation of the Muslim League. Mr. Jinnah was not willing to co-operate with us." He thus hinted that the Congress would now form the government without the League. About the changed attitude of the Viceroy, Nehru further stated in the same letter: "Your new proposal would change the whole approach to the problem and put an end to the responsibility which, at your suggestion, we had undertaken. We are now asked to revert to the previous stage which, we had thought, had finally ended after months of fruitless effort."[4]

Jinnah's attitude of Direct Action and the Great Calcutta-killing upset Wavell, who finally lost patience, remarking, that it was of no use to invite Jinnah to co-operate. But immediately after the tone of the Viceroy underwent a change went Nehru pressed him that the number of members in the new Cabinet should be raised to fifteen for an efficient administration and also of enabling the representative of the Anglo-Indian community to have a part in it. But the Viceroy, though he understood "the advantage of an Anglo-Indian representative in the Executive Council", objected to it on the ground that there must be a room for Muslim League joining the government, which seemed a matter of "paramount importance" to him.[5] The Viceroy thus

2. S. I. N. C., II, p. 805.
3. Pyarelal, *Mahatma Gandhi*, Vol. I, pp. 265-266.
4. Nehru's letter to Wavell, August 19, 1946 (Quoted in Dorothy, *Nehru*, Vol. II, pp. 244-245).
5. Pyarelal, *Mahatma Gandhi*, Vol. I, p. 266.

left no stone unturned for the League to join in the Interim Government. Nehru became vexed with Wavell; he took strong exception to this, doubting Wavell's move "again to please Jinnah". He became greatly dissatisfied for Wavell's attempt to appease the Muslim League when the latter had already refused to form the ministry. The joining of the Muslim League, according to Nehru would make the Central government ineffective and unstable. "That might lead to a worsening the situation" wrote Nehru to Wavell, "and possibly even to a repetition of the horrors of Calcutta".[6]

The failure of Nehru and Wavell to bring the League in the Interim Government enraged the former, who now announced the personnel of the Interim Government on August 24 from Viceroy's house. It consisted of 14 members out of which 12 names were announced, while the remaining two Muslims from the Congress were to be appointed later. It was decided to assume office on September 2. Accordingly, the members of the Governor-General's Executive Council were resigned and replaced by the Congress members to form the Interim Government. The Interim Government was to consist of Jawaharlal Nehru, Ballabhbhai Patel, Rajendra Prasad, Asaf Ali, C. Rajagopalachari, Sarat Chandra Bose, John Mathai, Baldev Singh, Shaffaat Ahmad Khan, Jagjivan Ram, Syed Ali Zaheer and C. H. Bhabha.[7] After announcing the names of the ministers on August 25, the Viceroy made a broadcast on the same day expressing his view of allowing the "maximum freedom" to the new government in the "day to day administration of the country". He described it a very momentous step on India's road to freedom. At the same time, he regretted the Muslim League for not joining in the coalition government, though 5 Muslim seats out of 12, were reserved for them and inspite of the assurances about the scheme of the Constitution-making according to procedure, had been promised. And on the eve of this announcement he again appealed them to join in the coalition by observing : "The Muslim

6. Nehru's letter to Wavell, August 22 (Dorothy, *Nehru* II, p. 245).

7. S. I. N. C., II, p. ccxxxiv.

League need have no fear of being outvoted on any essential issue. A coalition Government can only exist and function on the condition that both the main parties to it are satisfied. I will see that the most important portfolios are equitably shared. I sincerely trust that the League will reconsider their policy and decide to participate in the Government". In the same broadcast, he further remarked : "In spite of all immediate appearances, I believe there is yet a chance of agreement between the two principal parties. I am quite sure that there is a very large body of opinion in both parties and of non-party men who would welcome such an agreement, and I hope, they will all work for it". The Viceroy's main intention was to bring the League within the ministry. "Remember", he made an urgent call, "the Interim Government can be re-formed tomorrow if the League decided to come in". In case of any dispute, the Viceroy declared "that the Congress are ready to agree that any dispute or interpretation may be referred to the Federal Court."[8]

Jinnah's reply to this broadcast was sharply a denial. He charged the Viceroy as he had been drifted from truth. In his statement, Jinnah alleged : "The truth is that the Viceroy wrote to me on July 22 making certain proposals which were virtually and substantially different from the Interim Government proposals embodied in the statement of June 16 and the assurances given to the Muslim League." It was due to this, Jinnah stated "that though the assurances were given that the scheme of the Constitution-making would be worked in accordance with the procedure laid down, and though the new Interim Government is to operate under the existing constitution," it had not been possible for the League to join in the Coalition." In his statement, Jinnah also criticised the attitude of Nehru : "I had and have no knowledge or information as to what actually transpired between the Congress and the Viceroy but Pandit Jawaharlal Nehru, I suppose as arranged, came to see me on August 15. It was merely a formality and he made his offer : that the Congress were willing to give, out of fourteen, five seats to the Muslim League

8. The Viceroy's Broadcast, August 25 (*Ibid.*, pp. ccxxxv-ccxxxvi).

and the remaining nine were to be nominated by them including one Muslim of their choice; that he was not forming the Executive Council under the present constitution but a Provisional National Government responsible to the present Legislative Assembly." Jinnah added that Nehru "had no new suggestion to make," but to make conspiracy against the League. "Therefore", he remarked sarcastically, "the Viceroy, Pandit Nehru and the Congress leaders have now for nearly a week carried on their discussions and negotiations behind my back and without any knowledge or information being furnished to me except the communique that was issued last night announcing the formation of the Interim Government."[9]

After clarifying his stand on Viceroy's broadcast, Jinnah issued a general statement on August 27, narrating the reaction of the Muslim League : "My reaction to the Viceroy's broadcast is that he has struck a severe blow to the Muslim League and Muslim India, but I am sure that the Mussalmans of India will bear this up with fortitude and courage and learn lessons from our failure to secure our just and honourable position in the Interim Government and the Constituent Assembly." His "real freedom" could not be achieved without the division of Indian sub-continent "Of course, we are not opposed to the freedom of the peoples of India, and we have made it clear that the only solution of India's problem is a division of India into Pakistan and Hindustan, which would mean real freedom for the two major nations." About the reference of the Federal Court, in case of dispute, Jinnah stated that "there is no provision for such a dispute being referred to the Federal Court" and when the parties fundamentally differed in the interpretations regarding the basic terms, he believed that the Federal Court could solve no problem. "I am sorrier than the Viceroy," remarked Jinnah for failure "to secure a coalition Government," but if the Viceroy was "really sincere," let him present a concrete proposal; his earnest desire might be enforced "by his deeds and action."[10]

9. Jinnah's reply to the Viceroy, August 26 (*Ibid.*, pp. ccxxxvi-ccxxxvii).
10. Jinnah's statement, August 27 (*Ibid.*, pp. ccxl-ccxli).

After the announcement of the name of the Congress ministers in the Interim Government, Nehru felt the need of the formation of the Constituent Assembly. It could not be held up for long as because the League's refusal to join it or their creating disturbances in the country. Nehru commented that the work of the Constituent Assembly must proceed immediately without the League.[11] While Wavell agreed on Nehru's resentment he cautioned him not to make any haste. But Nehru continued to press his argument: "An indefinite postponement of it would not only be wrong in principle but would have harmful practical results even from the point of view of our gaining co-operation of the Muslim League which we desire."[12]

After prolonged controversy Congress decided to form the Interim Provisional Government and assumed office on September 2, 1946.[13] Jawaharlal Nehru became the Vice President of the Viceroy's Executive Council-*de facto* Prime Minister and member for External Affairs and Commonwealth Relations. On the same day, the Private Secretary to the Viceroy issued a directive prohibiting the ministers to visit any Indian State without prior information given to the Political department. The ministers were also debarred to make speeches of a "political nature" in the Indian states.[14] The Muslim League, on the other hand, became not only disappointed and enraged; but on the same day when Congress assumed office, it attempted to stage a demonstration in Delhi and elsewhere, though the attempts could not become successful.[15]

But the Congress assumption of office in the Interim Government disturbed Wavell. He took it as a feeling of defeatism

11. Nehru's letter to Wavell, August 28 (Dorothy, *Nehru* II, p. 246).
12. Pyarelal, *Mahatma Gandhi*, Vol. I, p. 270.
13. Among the twelve members of the Interim Government, Baldev Singh, Shaffaat Ahmed Khan, C. Rajagopalachari, John Mathai and C. H. Bhabha were not present at the swearing-in ceremony.
14. Pyarelal, *Mahatma Gandhi*, Vol. I, p. 273.
15. Azad, I. W. F. p. 175.

He called it a breakdown plan, as the Congress and the League could not come to an agreement. He did not want that the Congress should have wield power alone. He wanted the British to hand over the Hindu-majority provinces to Congress and to retain for himself the control over the Muslim majority provinces of North-West Frontier Province, Punjab, Sind, Bengal and Assam; until these provinces were able to evolve a Constitution for their own. Thus he modified his scheme on September 1 and decided to control over two Hindu-majority Provinces of Bihar and Uttar Pradesh to win the goodwill of the Muslim League. He placed his scheme all along, though could not become successful.[16] But the Viceroy was not discouraged by its non-acceptance. He tried to create further trouble. He now believed that the Congress acceptance of May 16 offer was not genuine. He was bent upon proving it, insisting the Congress to give a firm assurance that it would abide strictly by the scheme of compulsory grouping of provinces. Further, when Nehru considered himself responsible for vacant portfolios of the Government, Wavell insisted them the responsibility of the Viceroy. Nehru's stand was that the Interim Government would function as a Cabinet, jointly responsible for decisions; Wavell's thought was different. Wavell informed Nehru his intention to discontinue the practice of secretaries having direct access to him, but wished to meet the members of the government at regular intervals.[17]

When this type of mutual distrust started between Nehru and Wavell, the former made the position of the Interim Government clear in his broadcast on September 7 by remarking that it was a "stepping stone to the full independence of India", and that "we were yet on the march and the goal had still to be reached." According to him the freedom was "for all the people of India and not for any group or class or the followers of one religion. About the future Constitution of free India, Nehru observed that "the Interim National Government is part of a larger scheme which includes the Constituent Assembly which will meet soon to give shape to the Constitution of a free and independent India". It

16. Pandey, *Nehru*, pp. 269-270.
17. S. W. J. N., Vol. I, p. 149-150.

was for the early realisation of this goal of full independence, the Congress had entered in the government. Nehru further warned the nation to keep away from power politics of the groups and advocated for the colonial emancipation of the countries of the world. He also hoped that by this way the Constituent Assembly tangle might also be solved. He invited the co-operation of all by observing : "We shall go to the Constituent Assembly with the fired determination of finding a common basis for agreement on all controversial issues. And so, inspite of all that has happened and the hard words that have been said, we have kept the path of co-operation open, and we invite even those who differ from us to enter the Constituent Assembly as equals and partners with us with no binding commitments."[18]

In the inaugural address of the A. I. C. C. session held at New Delhi on September 23, Nehru relinquished the Congress Presidentship[19], remarking it "impossible for a person to hold office in the Interim Government and at the same time continue to be Congress President as well." He had before him the bigger responsibility of framing the future policy of India as the head of the government. Moreover the Congress had to wage another struggle for securing freedom. Thus on this issue that no one could hold both the offices, Govind Ballabh Pant's resolution that "no one will be debarred from the membership of the Working Committee or any other body of the Congress on account of his holding office in the Interim Government," was passed by a large majority of the A. I. C. C. on September 24. About the role of the Congress in the Interim Government, Nehru remarked : "The Congress has assumed a great responsibility in forming the Interim Government. We are there to construct a new edifice. And it is for the A. I. C. C. to help us in this task. The whole world is

18. Nehru's broadcast to the Nation, September 7, 1946. (S. I. N. C., Vol. II, pp. ccxlii-ccxliv). Also, Dorothy, *Nehru* II, p.284.
19. The Congress Working Committee accepted Nehru's resignation for Presidentship on September 25, but requested him to continue till the election of a new President.

watching the Congress and India. India cannot live in isolation, what happens elsewhere in the world affects us. Similarly the whole world will be affected by our policy."[20]

On the second day of the AICC session on September, 24, Nehru raised the question of relation between the members of the Interim Government *vis-a-vis* the Working Committee of the Congress. He observed that the five members of the Congress Working Committee[21] who had participated in the Interim Government as well, were ready to resign from either. Before Nehru party organisation was more important than the membership of the Interim Government. "If the choice was left to me and my four colleagues," Nehru remarked, "I am sure we would prefer membership of the Congress Working Committee to membership of the Interim Government. Personally, I would like to continue President of the Congress rather than become a member of the Government. But sometimes men are called upon to do things that give no personal pleasure but have to be undertaken as a duty." Nehru at least wanted to limit the proportion of members of the Interim Government who could be permitted to remain on the Working Committee. He therefore put to the vote a composite amendment seeking to limit the number of members of the Interim Government. But this resolution of Nehru was also rejected by an overwhelming majority of the Congress. On the question of Munshi Ahmed Din's contention that "independence cannot be achieved without a revolution" Nehru reacted sharply by replying, "May I ask, if we have not worked for revolution all these twenty-five years?" About the revolutionaries, he said: "Revolutionaries in other countries follow the method of breaking down the obstacles first and then rebuilding, whereas we in India under Mahatma Gandhi's guidance have succeeded in rebuilding, simultaneously with breaking down obstacles."[22]

20. S. W. J. N., Vol. I, pp. 3-4.
21. Jawaharlal Nehru, Ballabhbhai Patel, Rajendra Prasad, C. Rajagopalachari and Sarat Chandra Bose.
22. Nehru's speech on the Working Committee resolution at the A. I. C. C., New Delhi, September 24 (S.W.J.N., vol. I, pp. 5-6).

About the party organisation and work, Nehru believed that the Congress had immensely grown in strength particularly in two ways. It had increased hold over the masses and had cleared the obstacles in its way. But he believed that for India's independence, Muslim League was the major obstacle. And according to him the Congress had gained popularity but it had "not yet able to direct the course of events in the country. Whether it is a strike or a riot, the Congress is unable to control it. This makes it obvious that the Congress organisation has not yet adapted itself to the changed circumstances." His party wanted a Congress office in every village but according to Nehru the real problem was to change the outlook of the masses.[28]

During this period Wavell was bent upon bringing the Muslim League, as he believed it impossible to force Congress out of the government. He was warned by the Muslim League's Direct Action resulting in the Calcutta-Killing and realised a great disaster until a Congress-League Coalition government was formed at the Centre, and if possible, in the provinces as well. But the Congress leadership was opposed to the Muslim League being drawn into the government. The longer the League wes kept out of the power, the greater the opportunity of the Congress to strengthen its hold over administration. But Wavell always kept on insisting on the Congress and at the same time, negotiating with Jinnah, almost behind Nehru's back. And before Nehru, it was no matter how much he wished the exclusion of the League from the government, he could not take a firm stand on this issue. Nehru could not disregard his own conscience for securing political gains at the cost of his popularity.

During their negotiations, Jinnah expressed before Wavell his hope that the Congress would not appoint a nationalist Muslim to the Cabinet. He indicated his disapproval of the scheduled caste candidate as well and asked for safeguards for deciding major communal issues by a vote of both communities. Wavell assured him that in the event of a vacancy of minority

23. Nehru's speech about Party Organisation and work, September 24 (S, W. J. N., Vol. I, pp. 7-8).

seats both parties would be consulted. Jinnah insisted that if the controversy over the Grouping Clause was settled, only then the long-term issue could be decided by the League. Wavell agreed with Jinnah, provided Nehru responded favourably to the points of issue raised by the Muslim League.[24]

Wavell thus turned towards Nehru and had a meeting with him on September 26 for an hour. The Viceroy apprised Nehru the necessity of Muslim League's participation in the Interim Government as well as in the Constituent Assembly. Their talks centred round on the issue of nationalist Muslim. While the League insisted of being regarded as the sole representative of the Muslims in India, Nehru professed the Congress a natianalist body and not for the Hindus alone. So while Nehru was in no way prepared to forego this principle, Wavell thought it "wrong to throw an opportunity of a coalition on a comparatively minor issue."[25]

Wavell's talk with Jinnah bore some fruits and on October 4, he sent a copy of Jinnah's demands to Nehru "as the basis of the League's joining in the Interim Government."[26] Jinnah's demands included nine points were prepared on October 3, and were handed over to the Viceroy as under the following heads : 1. The Executive Council was to consist of 14 members. 2. The Congress might nominate 6 members including one from scheduled caste. 3. No Muslim was to be included within the Congress quota. 4. In case of conflict on communal basis no decision was to be taken. 5. Vice-President was to be nominated by rotation. 6. Representatives of minorities was to be chosen thereafter in consultation with the Congress and the Muslim League. 7. Important portfolios was to be equally distributed berween the Congress and the Muslim League. 8. Arrangements were not be be changed without agreement

---

24. S. W. J. N., Vol. I, p. 163.
25. Wavell's interview with Nehru, September 26 *Ibid.*, pp. 163-164).
26. *Ibid.*, p. 165. Also, Dorothy, *Nehru* II, p. 254.

of the two parties and 9. Long-term plan was to be postponed till agreements were reached and the Interim Government set up.[27]

Wavell in his reply to Nehru on October 4, agreed to four of Jinnah's nine points : 1, 2, 6 and 8. As regards Jinnah's other demands, Wavell believed that each party was free to nominate its representatives, while the communal issues might be decided by vote. He did not agree about the arrangement of rotational Vice-Presidents but in case of absence of the Governor-General and the Vice-President, he promised to nominate a Muslim League member to preside over the Cabinet He agreed on the equal distribution of important portfolios between the parties.[28]

During this period Nehru continued tirelessly in favour of a rational method of establishing a representative, united, independent and democratic government for India. In his letter to the Viceroy he emphasised great "importance to the Cabinet functioning as a team with responsibility". Nehru criticised Jinnah's point No. 2, whereln the latter mentioned that the six nominess of the Congress was to include one Scheduled Caste representative. And yet Jinnah further mentioned that "it must not be taken that the Muslim League has agreed to, or approves of, the selection of the Scheduled Caste representative". Nehru could not understand how tho question of agreement or approval by the League could be taken in regard to the nominees of the Congress.[29] About Jinnah's point No. 5, Nehru agreed, if it could help to find a solution, to a Muslim League member being chosen as Vice-Chairman of the Co-ordination Committee of the Cabinet. But Nehru personally felt that this question might introduce a new element of difficulty. If the Viceroy was to nominate a Muslim League member to preside over the Cabinet during the absence of the Governor-General and the Vice-President, such nomination

27. S. W. J. N., Vol. I, p. 165 f.n.
28. *Ibid.*
29. Wavell in his letter to Nehru and Jinnah on July 22, had already conceeded that six members including one scheduled caste representative would be nominated by the Congress.

by the Viceroy "would be neither constitutional nor otherwise desirable". This situation could only be tackled between the Congress and the League. About Jinnah's point No. 6, Nehru felt that if the Coalition was to function as a Cabinet, "the whole Cabinet should be consulted before any decision is arrived at". It was to interfere seriously on the development of the Cabinet system, "if the Governor-General consulted each group or individual member separately and then came to his own decision in the matter". Nehru led great stress for the Cabinet to function together and was not to be treated as consisting of separate groups. For this end in view, Nehru professed that "so far as we are concerned, we shall certainly do our utmost to resolve all differences of opinion by friendly discussions among the Cabinet members." On the other hand, he remarked in his note to the Viceroy : "If any procedure is adopted which encourages one group functioning within the Cabinet and encourages separate groups to function separately, this would seriously initiate against the whole conception of Cabinet Government." However, Nehru was anxious to remove obstacles in way of an agreement."[30]

Next day, on October 5, Nehru went to Jinnah, where he had a very full and friendly talk with him. The points raised by Jinnah in their conversation were :

1. Gandhiji suggested a formula to Jinnah.[31]
2. The League was not responsible for the members representing the scheduled castes and the minorities.

30. Nehru's letter to Wavell, October 4 (S. W. J. N., Vol. I, pp. 165-167; Dorothy, *Nehru*, II, pp. 254-255; Pyarelal, *Mahatma Gandhi*, I, pp. 278-279).

31. An agreement was signed on October 4 by Mahatma Gandhi on behalf of the Congress and the Nawab of Bhopal and Shoaib Qureshi for the Muslim League by which the Congress accepted the Muslim League as the sole representative of the Muslims of India. Gandhiji later declared that he would not ask the Working Committee to accept the formula.

3. What should be done in case of any vacancy should arise among the members representing the minorities other then the Scheduled Castes.
4. The procedure to be adopted over what may be called major communal issues; and
5. Alternating Vice-Presidentship.

After his talk with Jinnah, Nehru had discussed the issues with some of his Congress colleagues about the possibility of a repprochement. All agreed that "nothing could be happier and better for the country than that these two organisations should meet again......resolving all their differences by mutual consultation and never desiring the intervention of the British Government through the Viceroy". Therefore the Congress welcomed the decision of the League to join the Interim Government.

In his letter addressed to Jinnah, Nehru wrote that regarding point no. 1, "We feel that the formula is not happily worded." Congress was willing to accept the Muslim League as the "authoritative representative organisation of an overwhelming majority of the Muslims of India," provided "the League recognises the Congress as the authoritative organisation representing all non-Muslims and such Muslims as have thrown in their lot with the Congress." For this recognition, Nehru suggested that no formula was necessary. Regarding point No. 2, Nehru believed that the question of the League's responsibility did not arise at all, "as you do not raise any objections to the present constitution of the Government in this respect." Regarding point No. 3, Nehru was of opinion that in case of vacancy, the whole Cabinet was to consider what should be done to fill the vacancy and was to advise the Viceroy accordingly. Regarding point no. 4, Jinnah's suggestion about the Federal Court did not seem feasible. "Matters coming before the Cabinet cannot be made the subject matter of references to Court," remarked Nehru in his note to Jinnah. Regarding point No. 5, it was out of question to have any rotation in the Vice-Presidentship. The Congress had no objection, if the League desired to have an additional Vice-

Chairman for the Co-ordination Committee of the Cabinet.[32]

But on October 7 Nehru was surprised to receive a letter from Jinnah, which was at variance with the spirit of their whole talk. In that letter Jinnah wrote to Nehru that the latter's reply regarding point No. 1 "was accepted by Mr. Gandhi and me and the meeting between us was arranged on that basis...for the purpose of reconstituting the Interim Government." The formula that was put forward in the letter was as under : "The Congress does not challenge and accepts that the Muslim League now is the authoritative representative of an overwhelming majority of the Muslims in India. As such and in accordance with democratic principles they alone have to-day an unquestionable right to represent the Musiims of India. But the Congress cannot agree that any restriction or limitation should be put upon the Congress to choose such representatives as they think proper from amongst the members of the Congress as their representatives."[33] Now Jinnah accused Nehru in making changes and his rejection of the formula. "As the whole basis of our talk on another matters was the formula agreed to by Mr. Gandhi, I don't think we can make any further progress unless it is accepted by you as a basis upon which we can proceed to discuss other points," remarked Jinnah in his letter. Jinnah again repeated his nine points before Nehru with some modifications.

1. The total number of members of the Executive Council to be 14.

2. Six nominees of the Congress will include the scheduled caste representative, but it must not be taken that the Muslim League has agreed to, or approves of, the selection of the scheduled castes representative, the ultimate responsibility in that behalf being with the Governor-General and Viceroy.

3. That the Congress should not include in the remaining five members of their quota a Muslim of their choice.

---

32. Nehru's letter to Jinnah, October 6 (S. W. J. N., Vol. I, pp. 172-174; S. I. N. C., Vol. II, pp. ccliv-cclv).
33. In quoting the formula, Jinnah omitted the second paragraph.

4. Safeguard : that there should be a convention that on major communal issues, if the majority of Hindu or Muslim members of the Executive Council are opposed, then no decision should be taken.

5. Alternative or rotational Vice-President should be appointed in fairness to both the major communitios as it was adopted in the UNO Conference.

6. The Muslim League was not consulted in the selection of the three minority representatives, that is, Sikh, Indian Christian and Parsi. And it should not be taken that the Muslim League approves of the selection that has been made. But in future, in the event of their being a vacancy owing to death, resignation or otherwise, representative of these minorities should be chosen in consultation with the two major parties—the Muslim League and the Congress.

7. Portfolios : The most important portfolios should be equally distributed between the two major parties—the Muslim League and the Congress.

8. That the above arrangement should not be changed or modified unless both the major parties—the Muslim League and the Congress agree.

9. The question of the settlement of tho long-term plan should stand over until a better and more conducive atmosphere is created and an agreement has been reached on the points stated above and after the Interim Government has been re-formed and finally set up."[33]

Nehru was perturbed by Jinnah's letter which seemed to him at variance with the spirit of his talk. The other Congress leaders were also greatly disturbed by the list of points forwarded by Jinnah. Nehru and the other Congress leaders did not accept the formula agreed to by Gandhiji and Jinnah. Nehru put forward the paragraph of the formula that was omitted by Jinnah : "It is understood that all the ministers of the Interim Government will

33. S. I. N. C., vol. II, pp. cclv-cclvi.

work as a team for the good of the whole of India and will never invoke the intervention of the Governor-General in any case." Nehru further emphasised that the Congress had the right to appoint a Muslim out of its quota; and that the Congress position in regard to the Nationalist Muslims and the small minorities should not be challenged by the League. About Jinnah's suggestion that the Vice-President and the Leader of the Central Assembly should not be the same person, Nehru agreed that the Leader of the Central Assembly might be a Muslim League member of the Cabinet.[34]

Meanwhile the Viceroy assured Jinnah that the "Muslim League are at liberty to nominate any one they wish for their own quota of seats in the Cabinet," provided it was accepted by the Viceroy and His Majesty. After a long persuations and promises from the Viceroy, Jinnah at last agreed to join in the Interim Government. After fomenting distrust for what had already been made, Jinnah accepted the invitation and wrote to the Viceroy on October 13 :

"We consider and maintain that the imposition of this decision is contrary to the declaration of August 8, since, according to your decision we have a right to nominate five members of the Executive Council on behalf of the Muslim League." He argued that this decision had been taken by the League for the interests of the Muslims as it would be "fatal to leave the entire field of administration" in the hands of the Congress. Therefore the League had "decied to nominate five on behalf of the Muslim League" in the Interim Government.[35] This decision of the Muslim League was welcomed by the Viceroy who requested Jinnah to send the name of five Muslim representatives "to be submitted to His Majesty for approval."[36] The Viceroy informed this

34. Nehru's letter to Jinnah, October 8 (*Ibid,* cclvi-cclvii; S. W. J. N., Vol. I, pp. 174-175; Dorothy, *Nehru* II, pp. 257-258).
35. Jinnah's letter to the Viceroy, October 13 (S. I. N. C., Vol. II, p. cclxi).
36. Viceroy's letter to Jinnah, October 23 (*Ibid*).

decision of the League to Nehru on the same day.[37] Nehru wanted to know the name of the Muslim League members as well as the terms of inclusion of the League members in the Interim Government.[38] Nehru became disturbed as he did not know the terms on which the League agreed to join in the government. So on the next day, he wrote to Wavell another letter : "You made it clear that a Coalition Government must necessarily work as a team and not as a joining together of rival groups which did not co-operate for a common purpose......the basis for participation in the Cabinet must...be presumed to be the acceptance of the Cabinet Mission's statement of 16th May."[39]

As Nehru became very eager to know the attitude of the League on the eve of their joining in the Coalition government, he personally met the Viceroy with whom he had a long and "friendly" discussion. On Nehru's querry to know the name of the nominees of the League, Wavell did not divulge the names but replied that it was not for the cabinet to discuss the names, although Nehru had the right to consult his colleagues. When Nehru wanted to know the basis for which Jinnah was coming in, Wavell replied that his talk with Jinnah centred round on the matter of minority representatives. To this, Nehru pointed out "that Jinnah should not have any veto on the appointment of a representatative." When Nehru wanted to know whether Jinnah had accepted the long-term issue, Wavell replied that "Jinnah was prepared to call a meeting of his Council to reverse their Bombay decision as soon as he was satisfied that the statement of May 16th would be observed." On the question of the adjustment of portfolios, Nehru replied that the Congress had not yet decided which of the present members would make room for the League[40], but he was quite sure that the Congress would include a Nationalist Muslim in the government. Wavell then suggested that of the four main portfolios, Defence, External Affairs, Home and Finance, it was generally agreed that Mathai should remain

37. Nehru's letter to Jinnah, October 13 (*Ibid.*, p. cclvIII).
38. Nehru's letter to Wavell, October 13 (S. W. J. N., Vol. I, p. 180).
39. Pyarelal, *Mahatma Gandhi*, Vol. I, pp. 282-283.

in charge of Finance. So out of remaining three, the Viceroy stressed the League must have one. The Viceroy also supported Baldev Singh in charge of Defence, and Nehru—in charge of External Affairs. Nehru replied that it would be very difficult to shift Patel from Home Ministry. The Viceroy then suggested that the League might either accept Commerce or Industries and Supplies.[41]

On October 14, Jinnah forwarded to Wavell the names of five nominees on behalf of the Muslim League. They were, (1) Liaqat Ali Khan—Honorary Secretary, All India Muslim League, (2) I. I. Chundrigar—Leader of the Muslim League in Bombay Legislative Assembly. (3) Abur Rab Nishtar—member, Working Committee of the Muslim League, (4) Ghaznafar Ali Khan—member All-India Muslim League Council, and (5) Jogendra Nath Mandal—a minister of the Bengal Government.[42]

As suggested by the Viceroy, Nehru provided five places for the Muslim League nominees in his Cabinet. Out of 14 seats in the Interim Government only 12 were filled, leaving scope for two new appointments. And so the Congress decided, with the consent of the ministers, that three of them, namely Sarat Chandra Bose, Shaffaat Ahmad Khan and Syed Ali Zaheer should retire. Nehru wished that after his return from the Frontier[43], the question of dividing the portfolios should be considered. He did not want to create any disturbance in the present arrangements but he feared "disturbance is inevitable." It seemed to him undesirable to reshaffle any portfolios as the ministers "have been doing good work and it would be unfair to make any change". Nehru stressed that the present portfolios of Sardar

40. Before finalising the decision, Nehru wanted to consult Sarat Chandra Bose.
41. Wavell's interview with Nehru, October 14 (S. W. J. N., Vol. I, pp. 181-183).
42. Jinnah's letter to the Viceroy, October 14 (S. I. N. C., II, pp. cclxi-cclxii).
43. Nehru's tour on the North-West Frontier Province began on October 16.

Patel would remain with him. "At the present moment to ask Sardar Patel to leave his portfolio would be an act of extreme discourtesy to him," remarked Nehru in his note. The Congress ministers who had voluntarily retired" have justified their selection in every way" and so Nehru regrettably noted that "I should have to part with them in this way". On the other hand, the Congress did not raise any objection to the names proposed by League. The League had the freedom to nominate five persons according to their choice. But Nehru suspected their dubious role. The choice of the League indicated their desire "to have conflict rather than to work in co-operation", which was indicative of their nomination to a Scheduled Caste candidate. Nehru feared that "the standard of the Cabinet will be much lowered by their association."[44] Still Nehru wished to carry on the work "in a spirit of team-work", believing at the same time that "our work in future will not be easy."[45]

Muslim League joined the Interim Government on October 15, 1946; Nehru was aware of the danger of such a coalition, but he had no power to change the course of events.

---

44. About this nomination of the League, Azad observed: "Mr. Jinnah acted in a most peculiar manner. Khwaja Nazimuddin and Nawab Ismail Khan had never taken an extreme position in the disputes between the Congress and the League. This had obviously displeased Jinnah. He thought that they would not be yes men and he therefore decided to exclude them from his list."—Azad, I. W. F. p. 176.
45. Nehru's two letters to the Viceroy on October 15 (S. W. J. N., Vol. I, pp. 185-187).

CHAPTER–V

NEHRU'S FOREIGN POLICY OF CO-OPERATION AND NON-ALIGNMENT

The coming of the Labour Government in power aroused high hopes in Jawaharlal Nehru, believing that like Churchill, it did not stand on the way of the emancipation of India. Immediately after his release from prison, between July 1945 to March, 1946, Nehru nourished his optimism on hopes for his contact with the people of India. He believed that colonisation had to retreat from Asia soon after the conclusion of the war. Accordingly he visualised a new world and a large federation of countries emerging on the map of the world. India had the potential and strategic importance of being the centre of South and South-East Asia. He visualised for a world federation. The enthusiasm, inspiration and the honour that he had received from his contact with the masses, made him rather visionary.

But from September 2, 1946, when the Interim Government was first constituted, Nehru became increasingly frustrated as a nationalist and found inspiration in laying down the basic structure of a free India. The Interim periad was of great importance to him, for he believed the emergence of a new structure of free India. Nehru lauched his foreign policy moving a resolution in the Constituent Assembly in December, 1946, emphasising his principle of friendliness towards all nations-particularly America, Soviet Union and China. He advocated the policy of non-alignment with either of the two major groups, the American and Russian, into which the world was then divided. Though America had a major role in international affairs but Nehru found more reason on the side of Russia. While addressing Indian delegates[1] to the United Nations General Assembly, Nehru emphasised his non-alignment policy.

---

1. Indian delegates in the U. N. O. were led by Mrs. Vajaylaxmi Pandit, Krishna Menon and K. P. S. Menon.

"If Russia helps us and speaks for us, it is right for us to express our gratitude and our friendliness. Not to do so for fear offending America or England or of losing some votes would be to become totally ineffective and untrue to ourselves."[2] The object of his foreign policy was to secure an impoıtant place in Asia, removing colonialism in Asian countries, friendship and co-operation with the neighbouring countries and the policy of non-alignment within the major powers of the world. With this end in view, he left no stone unturned. He visited different countries and began to spıead among the people his faith on friendship, co-operation and non-alignment.

From the beginning of 1946, Nehru began to send messages to different Asian countries, professing India's friendship and co-operation. After the defent of Japan, Nehru analysed the views of India and her attitude with the former country.[3] Before the war, the Indians looked up to the Japanese with admiration for their great achievements. Japan resembled very closely to India as it becamo a prey of aggressive western powers. But whenever Japan had adopted an attitude of the "Champions of Asiatic freedom", resulting in their "lust for domination and imperialist expansion" and the conquest of the Asian countries, the attitude of India on Japan began to change. During this period, Japan deprived Korea her freedom, China began to be harrassed, threatened and attacked. Thus the old admiration of India was replaced by resentment, India became the sympathisier of China for Japan's frequent attacks. This imperialistic adventure of Japan had been met with disaster after he end of the war. Now Japan must give up her old dreams of conquest and expansion. She should neither think in terms of revenge, for there was no end of hatred and revenge. But at the same time, Nehru admired Japan by observing : "The Japanese have shown extraordinary qualities which were turned in a wrong direction." So Nehru advised Japan to build the nation on sounder foundation

2. Nehru's letter to Vijaylaxmi Pandit, November 14, 1946 (Mrs. Pandit Paper).
3. Nehru was requested by Japaness Newspapers to express Indian attitude towards Japan after World War II.

and for achieving this end, "they must reject militarism and imperialism, and make of Japan a country of free democratic institution, which threatens none, and is feared by none". He further advised Japan "to build their economic order on the basis of equality and equal opportunities for all their people and not aiming at economic domination of any other country." This would create a prosperous and progressive Japan on friendly terms with her neighbouring Asian countries. Japan must regain the goodwill of China. The peace of the Far East depended on the co-operation of China and Japan. If Japan would adopt this attitude of friendship, India would surely join hands with Japan in the furtherance of Asiatic freedom.[4]

Nehru felt the need of uprooting the British Empire for the end of colonialism from Asian countries. "It is not an easy matter to refashion the destiny of hundreds of millions of people", observed Nehru during his speech on March 3, 1946. The world was growing faster "to lead to numerous upsets, which might take sometime to establish a new equilibrium on a surer foundation". This foundation could be laid for friendly co-operation between the opponents of yesterday. He believed that the "only hope for the world lies in co-operation and interdependence and the building up of a new world order of free nations". About the colonial problem of India, Nehru observed : "India is inevitably the crux of the colonial problem by virtue of her size and population, her millennia of cultured life, her contributions to civilization, her capacity and vast resources, her potential power and her strategic position. Historically she has been during the one hundred and fifty years the classic land of colonial imperialism".[5]

Nehru believed that the freedom of many other countries depended largely on the freedom of India. The British could not make excuses for the postponement of India's independence.

---

4. Nehru's message to Japan, January, 1946.
   (Vide, Bright, J. S., *Before and After Independence*, New Delhi, 1950, pp. 383-384.)
5. Quoted in Dorothy, *Nehru*, II, pp. 210-211.

He warned that the delay of India's freedom "will lead to conflict and disaster." He pointed out the case of Indonesia which was "witnessing a clear case of a shattered imperialism trying to hold on with the help of another imperialist power". Indonesia was well capable of looking after itself, with the support of its own people, if the outsiders were not permitted to intervene. The British role in Indonesia harmed that nation. But one day, the independence of Indonesia must be accepted and the popular government recognised. It was the case with Indo-China as well. This principle must be applied "in all Asian countries under subjection.,,. When the Asian countries would come out from bondage, Nehru believed that "a free India will link together the Middle East and China." For her strategic importance, "India is so situated as to form the centre of a group of Asian nations for defense as well as trade and commerce". About India's friendly tie with Asian countries, Nehru observed that India's "Cultural contacts with all these countries dates back thousands of years." But the end of colonialism and imperialism would not mean the splitting up of the world into a host of additional national states. After independence of all Asian nations, Nehru visualized a new grouping of all nations that would develop a new outlook of co-operation. This would lead to one world "which wise statesmen have dreamed and which seems to be the inevitable and only outcome of our present troubles."[6]

Nehru witnessed a great political awakening in South-East Asia, which was practically the same of India's aspiration for freedom from foreign rule.[7] He undertook a tour to these countries to apprise the people about the feeling of the Indians. In March 1946, while travelling to these countries, Nehru discussed various issues involving India,s freedom.

In his trip to South-East Asia, Nehru reached Singapore and made a public speech on March 18, remarking that India had

6. Quoted in Dorothy, *Nehru* II, pp. 212-213, From the *New York Times Magazine*, March 3, 1946.
7. It was during this time, in March 1946, Nehru's *The Discovery of India*, written while in jail, had been published.

become a burden for England as the possession of India gradually ceased to be of any profit for the British. While exclaiming India's freedom a reality, he observed : "There are strong forces at work to-day which are forcing England to recognize the freedom of India. Most intelligent people realise that freedom cannot be held back." He was hopeful for the satisfactory result that might emerge from the forthcoming Cabinet Mission talk. Nehru clarified India's stand by stating that India did not want freedom for her own self. She wanted freedom of all colonies. A world could not remain "half free and half slave". After India's freedom, Nehru exclaimed that "every ounce of her energy shall be used for the freedom of all subjected nations."[8] He also classified the stand of the Congress in its relation with the Muslim League. He described Jinnah neither a revolutionary, nor had the capacity to summon a revolt. Jinnah was fighting against Congress stand for self-determinatian. The Congress wanted autonomy of the federal units and did not want to compel any unit to stay within the Federation if by a free vote any unit decided to stay outside. But at the same time "no well-defined area of a unit can be compelled to join the seceding unit against the desires of the people living in that area."[9]

Narrating India's role in South-East Asia, Nehru stated at Kuala Lumpur that "India is going to play a big part." The historical tradition as well as her geographical position would compel India to play an important role. Nehru reminded : "If you think of the Middle East you must think of what is happening in India. If you think of South-East Asia you must consider what is happening in India." About India's relation with China he said : "India must be closely associated with China, otherwise unfortunate consequences might be the outcome." But Nehru did not fear any clash with China because India had, during thousands of years, an intimate contact with China. As both the countries had a common culture, during these thousands of years, there had been no cause for conflict. Thus India was to co-operate with

8. Bright, *Importent Speeches,* II, p. 480.
9. *Amrita Bazar Patrika,* March 23, 1946.

China. "But this co-operation between India and China is not going to be an aggressive co-operation against anybody else", remarked Nehru, assuring that this co-operation would bring peace in Asia and all over the world.[10] Nehru stressed the need of India's good neighbouring relation with China. China with a mighty past, had been a friend of India through ages. He hoped for a united and democratic China, playing a great part in future for the promotion of world peace and progress.[11]

Nehru was a great optimist for the future of India. After the formation of the Interim Government on September 2, he made a broadcast to the Nation visualising India's participation in international conferences as a free nation with her own policy "and not merely a satellite of another nation." He hoped to develop a close and direct contact with other nation and "to co-operate with them for the furtherance of world peace and freedom." As the head of the Interim Government, Nehru again stressed the need of co-operation with Asian countries by remarking that "The people of Asia are nearer and closer to us than others." Nehru wanted to cultivate friendship and co-operation with South-East and Middle East Asian countries. He pointed out : "India is so situated that she is the pivot of Western, Southern and South-East Asia. In the past her culture flowed to all these countries. They came to her in many ways. These contacts are being renewed and future is bound to see a closer union between India and South-East Asia on the one side and Afghanisthan, Iran and the Arab world on the other. To the furtherance of that close association of free countries we must devote ourselves. India was followed with anxious interest the struggle of the Indonesians for freedom and to them we send our good wishes."

In a press conference held on September 27, Nehru stressed about the attainment of India's full international status when India should establish entact with all the great nations of the

10. *Ibid.*, March 28, 1946.

11. Nehru's broadcast to the Nation, September 7, 1946 (S. I. N. C., II, pp. ccxlii-ccxliv.)

world and "that her relations with neighbouring countries in Asia should become still closer." He also felt the need of India's good relations with her neighbours. "So far her near neighbours are concerned" Nehru continued his remark in the press conference "India will watch with close interest the development of events in Palestine, Iran, Indonesia, China, Siam and Indo-China, ...with the aspiration of the peoples of these lands for the attainment of internal peace, freedom and their due place in the comity of nations."[12]

Nehru addressed the students and accademicians of the Calcutta University[13] narrating the future of India, not only with respect of independence, "but also the elder-sisterly relationship with all countries round about it". He reminded the youth that the centre of the world was shifting from Europe to Asia and India was to play a big part in world affairs. The world was passing through an extra-ordinary crisis in human affairs. But there had been hardly any time in the course of history when humanity had faced such a possibility of changes. "There must be a refashioning of the whole structure", warned Nehru, "if we are to prevent war and have peace." The two big wars in recent times, were the records of such failure. Nehru believed that this crisis was not only political and economic, but also psychological, for which the world was "going through a deep spiritual crisis." That spiritual crisis pervaded the whole of Asia; as a result Europe became dominant over Asia. So "in the last two hundred years Europe played a prominent part in world history not merely by force of arms but by virtue of its thoughts, its science and many other factors." So long Asia became utterly static and unchanging and as a result, the centre of the world events was shifting from Europe to America and partly to Asia. In his optimism, Nehru visualised Asia gradually regaining her

---

12. Nehru's Press Conference, September 27 (*Ibid.*, pp. ccxiv-ccxlvi).
13. Nehru's address to the students of Calcutta University, March 9 (A. B. P., March 10, 1946).

vitality and would be "coming back to what it was some hundreds of years ago."

Nehru believed that India should stand for peace. A new India should play a very important role, so as to form a connecting link between the various parts of Asia—The Middle East and the South East. But he was sure that "the British Empire in India is fading away." And in that situation, India was to function according to its own ability and strength. Nehru's vision of free India was something more than political freedom. He expressed his belief by observing : "It is a freedom in which four hundred million people can live the life which man should live......in which every individual shall have the door of opportunity open to him, in which every person will be provided with the necessities of life." Besides these minimum requirements of the people, he called upon the intellectuals of the country to explore the regions of science and start a great field of adventure.[14]

The object of Nehru's foreign policy was to establish the importance of Asia in world politics and to make India a natural focal point of pride. This aspect of Nehru's policy found expression at the first Asian Relations Conference held on March 23, 1947. He again referred to the glory of Asia, where the human civilization sprang up much earlier and where "the mind of man searched unceasingly for truth and the spirit of man ......lighted up the whole world."[15] As India was chosen as the venue of the Conference, it was befitting for her, as India for centuries became a meeting-point for all. He was convinced that the co-ordination of various countries of Asia was not only possible but exceedingly necessary. The question of an Asiatic Federation might be premature, "but some kind of closer association between these countries is necessary, both for defence and for trade purposes." There was a common feeling in Egypt in the West and Indonesia in the East, which would bring them closer to each other. But Nehru believed that this closer friend-

14. Quoted in Dorothy, *Nehru*, II, pp. 213-216
15. Jawaharlal Nehru's Speeches, 1946-64, Vol. I (Government of India Publication, 1949-69), p. 298.

ship among the Asian countries was in no way be anti-European. "The long-oppressed nations of Asia will inevitably seek to protect themselves by holding together as for as possible, and presenting a joint front in the Council of the World", remarked Nehru on the question of co-operation among Asian countries. The problems of Asian countries were more or less similar. The countries were urgently in need of defence, removal of the feudal structures and the establishment of democratic institutions. In the solution of the problems of development of industry and agriculture and the raising the standard of the masses, these countries might seek co-operation with the rest of the world.[16]

Nehru not only advocated the need for co-operation among the Asian countries, but also felt for friendship of the world at large. His policy of non-alignment had been developed from this principle. He wanted that the world should be safe from any danger. In his message to the United Nations, he observed: "If the Axis power had won the war, their victory would have been disastrous for freedom and democracy throughout the world." But the victory of the Allied Powers was a "victory in war and not in peace." This victory could not bring peace as other big problems await solution. On the other hand, Nehru believed that if the Allied power could pursue a different course, the duration of the war might had been lessened considerably. In that case, he predicted that consequence "would have been infinitely better for the whole world." But the war destroyed that chance "at a cost of millions of lives and infinite suffering." He further believed that the atomic energy could solve no problem of peace, rather it would increase "world conflict and destruction on a colossal scale." As a result, the whole world might turn either a free association of nations or be dominated by big power.[17]

Nehru also stressed the problems of the apartheid, the so called coloured races of Afro-Asian Countries. After his return

16. Bright, *Important Speeches*, I, pp. 384-385.
17. Ibid.

from the South-East Asian countries, he viewed the problems of South Africa and expressed his concern by stating : "We are not going to tolerate, and we are going to face all the consequences of opposing that policy, not only in South Africa, but in Asia as a whole, and in the world, because it raises a fundamental racial issue which applies to all Asians and Africans." As long as this issue was not solved, "it is going to be a menace to the peace of the world." The United Nations organisation would "be an absurdity if it tolerates racialism of this type", affirmed Nehru in his statement. The 'Nazi doctrine' should not be allowed to grow in South Africa. Nehru warned the big power by stating : "If the U. N. O, Europe or America do not do that, the time will soon come when all Asia may do, and so might Africa—where South Africa is situated.[18] He believed that the big powers were responsible for creating wars. "The big Powers are continuing the old imperiatist game, which already has led to two world wars," continued Nehru with due caution by remarking, "they have not learned anything from the tragic history of the past and, if they do not learn soon......they will plunge again into disaster."[19]

Nehru professed India's whole-hearted co-operation and unreserved support to the U. N. O. in both spirit and letter. For this purpose, India was to participate fully in its various activities and try to play a vital role in its council for her geographical position, population and her contribution towards peaceful progress. India was to make it clear that she would stand for the independence of all colonies and their full right to self-determination. In the U. N, O., India was to fight for the liberation of South Africa. In his view, "The treatment of Indians in South Africa is fundamentally a moral and human issue which...the General Assembly cannot disregard." In the U. N. O., the India's delegation was to oppose on point of principle, the Union of South Atrica's wish to absorb the Mandated Territory of South-

18. Nehru's statement on South Africa, April 5, 1946 (B.A.I., p. 259).
19. Nehru in an interview with Associated Press, Bombay, March 15, 1946.

West Africa. About the privilege of veto enjoyed by the Five Great Powers in the Security Council or the "rule of great power unanimity", Nehru believed that although on principle "India cannot take such an essentially undemocratic provision in the charter", but considering the world situation India "attaches the greatest importance to the continuance of great power unanimity and co-operation within the framework of the United Nations and would do nothing to prejudice that position".[20]

Nehru had always great sympathy for African aspirations of political freedom and economic advancement. He was opposed to the South-African racial differences. During the forties, he was becoming increasingly aware that Asia and Africa must make common cause for freedom and equality. In a letter to the African leaders, Nehru observed : "We have long struggled for the freedom and independence of India", but this freedom had a common heritage for all, more especially for those who had been deprived from freedom. He further clarified that India would always "stand and work for this wider freedom". India was particularly interested in the people of Africa. Nehru assured the African leaders the help of India by observing : "You can rest assured that the voice of India will always be raised in the cause of African freedom". In the coming Inter-Asian Relations Conference scheduled to be held at New Delhi, Nehru professed that "we should do for developing closer relations between Asia and Africa".[21]

Inspite of India's past history of conflict, Nehru hoped that an Independent India would have a friendly and co-operative relations with England and the countries of the British commonwealth. He expressed his view to the people of America by proclaiming : "We send our greetings to the people of the United States of America to whom destiny has given a major role in

---

20. Nehru's Press Conference on India's Foreign Policy, September, 27. (Dorothy, *Nehru*, II, pp. 265-269).
21. Letter to African Leaders, September 27 (*Ibid*, p. 270).

international affairs. We trust that this tremendous responsibility will be utilised for the furtherance of people and human freedom everywhere." He also greeted the other great nations of the modern world, particularly to Soviet Union : "The Soviet Union, which also carries a vast responsibility for shaping world events, we send greeting. They are our neighbours in Asia and inevitably we shall have to undertake many common tasks and have much to do with each other."[22]

Nehru's call for the regeneration of India was momentous : "India is on the move and the old order passes. Too long have we been passive spectators of events, the playthings of others. The initiative comes to our people now and we shall make the history of our choice. Let us all join in this mighty task and make India, the pride of our heart, great among nations, foremost in the arts of peace and progress. The door is open and destiny beckons to all. There is no question of who wins and who losses, for we have to ge forward and together as comrades and either all of us win or we all go down together. But there is going to be no failure. We go forward to success, to independence and to the freedom and well-being of the four hundred millions of India."[23]

On the very first day of his inaugural speech as the leader of the Interim-Government, Nehru made his policy clear about India's non-alignment policy : "We shall take full part in International Conferences as a free nation", he emphatically declared, "in the furtherance of world peace and freedom." He further cautioned the people of India about the Great Powers : "We propose, as far as possible, to keep away from power politics of groups aligned against one another which have led in the past two world wars." Thus he advocated for an independent foreign

22. Nehru's inaugural broadcast as *de facto* Prime Ministers, September 7, 1946. (*Ibid*, pp. 208-251). Also S. I. N. C. Vol. II, p. ccxliii.
23. Gunther, John, *Inside Asia* (New York, 1939), pp. 339-343.

policy. He added that "India will uphold the principle of freedom for dependent peoples and will oppose racial discrimination wherever it may occur. She will work with other peace-loving nations for international co-operation and goodwill without exploitation of one nation by another." For the attainment of India's full international status, Nehru added "India should establish contact with all the great nations of the world and that her relations with neighbouring countries in Asia should become still closer."[24]

---

24. S. I. N. C., vol. II, pp. ccxlii-ccxlv.

CHAPTER–VI

CONGRESS-LEAGUE CONTROVERSY AND THE LONDON CONFERENCE

The coalition Interim-Government was born in an atmosphere of suspicion and distrust. The Muslim League had no intention of working in co-operation with the Congress. On the very first day the League stated firmly : "We are going into the Interim Government to get a foothold to fight for our cherished goal of Pakistan." According to them the Interim-Government was a front of the Direct Action Compaign. Though a few of Jinnah's demands had been met but in the Interim-Government he wanted to demonstrate that the two communities could not function in harmony and that Pakistan was the only solution of this impasse.[1] It was perhaps another crucial moment in the history of India's freedom. On both moral and practical grounds the Congress leadership was opposed to the Muslim League. Congress now could not conceed the League's demand for Pakistan and two Constituent Assemblies.[2]

Nehru and the Congress leaders felt that Muslim League's joining in the Interim Government was to oppose every act of the Congress ministers. In a tone of despair Nehru wrote to Wavell that the Congress had not raised any objection to the names proposed by the Muslim League, though it was clear that the League desired a conflict rather than to work in co-operation. Past experiences of the Congress did not rely them on vague promises of the League.[3] "It is desirable" wrote Nehru to Wavell "to know exactly where we stand."[4]

---

1. Connell, John, *Auchinleck-A Critical Biography* (London, 1959), pp. 849-850.
2. S. I. N. C., Vol. II, p. 811.
3. Pyarelal, *Mahatma Gandhi*, Vol. I, p. 283.
4. Nehru's letter to Wavell, October 15 (MBN, p. 323).

In his reply to Nehru's letter, Wavell, who had developed meanwhile, a secret sympathy for the League, wrote to Nehru assuring "I have made it clear to Mr. Jinnah that the Muslim League's entry into the Interim Government is conditional on the acceptance of the scheme of May 16th......and that he must call his Council at an early date to agree to this." In the same tone Wavell communicated Jinnah's assurance of co-operation to Nehru : "As I have told you, Mr. Jinnah has assured me that the Muslim League will come into the Interim Government and the Constituent Assembly with the intention of co-operating." The Vieeroy, at the same time, advised Nehru to parts with one to the League out of External Affairs, Home and Defence, to accommodate them in the Government. He further wanted to know from Nehru "which of these portfolios you advise should be given to the League."[5]

Now Nehru began to judge the situation which, out of these three portfolios should be given to the Muslim League. So far as the portfolio of External Affairs was concerned, there were some essential points which should be cleared up first before parting that important office to the League. Jinnah was willing to join in the government provided the portfolio of External Affairs was given to him. But Nehru was unwilling to part with that important post, neither did he want it to rotate between Congress and the League. He considered that post like that of a Prime Minister and believed that a Congress leader alone should be entitled to hold it, as to create in future, a strong central government of independant India. On the other hand, Jinnah was prestige-conscious, not to occupy a position subordinate to Nehru. About parting with the other portfolios, Nehru wrote to Wavell that it "would be an entirely wrong step, leading to most unfortunate consequences, if any change was made in the portfolios of Defence and Home."[6]

5. Wavell's letter to Nehru, October 23 (Pyarelal, *Mahatma Gandhi* I, pp. 285-286).
6. Nehru's letter to Wavell, October 23 (*Ibid*, p. 286)

It was decided by the Viceroy that Home Portfolio should be given to the League. But on this issue, Nehru informed the Viecroy that "Patel would rather resign than continue in the cabinet if his portfolio was tampered with." This reshaffling of portfolios seemed most disgusting to Nehru and the Congress leaders. "Patel to leave his portfolio would be an act of extreme discourtesy to him," remarked Nehru sarcastically, observing: "He had been made a special target of attack by the official organ of the Muslim League and it becomes therefore, still more unbecoming for us to ask him to leave this portfolio."[7]

Nehru expressed satisfaction to Wevell about Jinnah's assurances to the latter in joining the Interim-Government and Constituent Assembly with the intention of co-operation. But still there remained another point and Nehru wanted to clearify from Wavell by informing : "While you have made this clear to Mr. Jinnah, it is not equally clear what the League's view is on this subject."[8] Past experiences of the Congress was much bitter if any matter left vague. So it would be very much unfortunate if the Congress did not clarify the position completely before starting the new experiment.[9]

From the correspondances of Nehru-Wavell-Jinnah and the acceptance of League's joining in the Interim Government clearly demonstrated the League's willingness of accepting the longterm scheme of the Cabinet Delegation's statement of May 16. It was pointed out then that a formal decision of the League would have been taken by the Council of the League, as they had originally passed the resolution of non-acceptance. But at the same time, the Working Committee of the League recommended the acceptance of this schemo. It was so long on this basis, the Congress proceeded with the League. Nehru therefore suggested that

7. *Ibid*, p. 286. Sardar Patel was in charge of Home, Information and Broadcasting ministries.
8. *Ibid*.
9. *Ibid*, p. 284.

"these two points should be cleared up."[10] It became not clear up to that time about the attitude of the League in regard to the long-term arrangement. However, this much was clear before the Congress that League's "Working Committee have not agreed to accept the statement of May 16th unless something further happens."[11] "The League's acceptance of the long-term scheme as embodied in the statement of May 16", Nehru informed Wavell, that was subjected only "to a formal ratification by the Council of the League at an early date." If their clarification was satisfactory, Nehru believed that the question of allotment of the portfolios could only be taken into consideration. "The second cannot proceed first, for it is dependent upon it and governed by it," Nehru stated emphatically to Wavell. Nehru believed that this clarification was necessary "in order to avoid future trouble." Nehru thought it very necessary because the League had consented to join with the Interim-Government not with an agreement with the Congress. Still Nehru welcomed their coming, but that coming would have little value or "might even be harmful to all concerned if it was really a prelude to inner as well as outer conflicts."[12]

As bitter question on allocation of portfolios and their reshaffling was going on for accomodating the League members, Nehru became greatly perturbed. When the situation was further drifting towards crisis, Nehru expressed his willingness to resign for the termination of the present Interim-Government. In a tone of despair, Nehru informed Wavell : "We cannot continue in the Government if a decision is imposed upon us against our will." It was not due to the allocation of portfolios to the League members, "but for the implications and circumstances...which compel us to do so." This question did not arise when Nehru was asked to form the Interim-Government two months ago.

10. Gwyer, Maurice and A. Appadorai, *Speeches and Documents on the Indian Constitution, 1921-47*, Vol. II (London, 1957), pp. 653-654.
11. Pyarelal, *Mahatma Gandhi*, I, p. 284.
12. G. I. C., Vol. II, p. 654.

This was done after much negotiations with the approval of His Majesty's Government. But under new crisis, termination of the present government seemed inevitable to him. Thus Nehru requested the Viecroy to inform all developments to His Majesty's Government'[13] in England. But Wavell was not prepared for this. His desire was to bring the League into the Government by any means. So he capitulated on the question of portfolios and the Congress continued in office[14] as usual.

Wavell's suggestion of parting one portfolio to the League, particularly the Home, created a surcharged atmosphere for the refusal of Patel. It was then Rafi Ahmed Kidwai who suggested to offer finance portfolio to the League, believing it a highly technical subject which no Muslim League member could handle effectively. On this proposal, Patel became greatly juvilent and gave his strongest support. Many of the Congress leaders including Patel believed that the League would not be able to manage finance.[15] But there was different repurcassion on the League. Finance portfolio, they thought was a marked victory for the League, which they could not expect from the Congress. With the control of finance department the League would have voice in every department of the government. Liaqat Ali soon became the finance minister. With the passage of time, the Congress soon realised their folly, repenting to allow that portfolio to the League. Now Sardar Patel also realised that he was playing into the hands of the League. Whatever proposal Patel made was either rejected or modified by Liaqat Ali. The League's persistance interference in the matter of finance, made it difficult for fhe Congress members to function effectively. With the help of the League, Liaqat Ali was able to reject or delay every proposal of the Congress. Soon "Sardar Patel discovered that

---

13. Nehru's letter to Wavell, October 24 (Dorothy, *Nehru*, II, p. 263).
14. Pyarelal, *Mahatma Gandhi*, Vol. I, p. 286.
15. It was Azad who did not like that finance which "was the key to Government", should be given to the League.

though he was Home Minister he could not create the post of a *Chaprasi* without Liaqat Ali's concurrence".[16]

Members of the League, at last, on the request of the Viecroy (and not from the invitation of Nehru—the leader of the Coalition Government) undertook the oath of secrecy in the Interim Government on October 26.[17] The Viecroy then informed Jinnah that he could offer the Muslim League, besides finance, the portfolios of Commerce, Posts and Air, Health and Legislature. So the Vieeroy wanted to know how these portfolios could be distributed among the Muslim League representatives in the Cabinet.[18] To Jinnah, the distribution was not equitable, still he agreed to them and did not "go into the matter further". With the consent of Jinnah the portfolios were distributed among the members of the League as under : Finance—Liaqat Ali Khan; Commence—I. I. Chundrigar; Posts and Air—A. R. Nishtar; Health–Ghaznafar Ali Khan and Legislature—Jogendra Nath Mandal.[19] The Viecroy announced these new appointments on October 27.

The Interim Government was formed in an atmosphere of suspicion and distrust between the contending parties. Suspicions preceeded before the formation, brought a great deal of mental strain afterwards. Nehru's hope was gradually taking shape in despair. "We formed the Interim Government with a particular object in view", Nehru wrote to Wavell, but "If that object leads into the background, then no particular purpose is served by our continuing in the Government." His idea was to function as a team in a Cabinet but that idea had totally been ignored, instead, it had been "stated openly by our new colleagues in the Government that they do not subscribe to this approach of ours."[20] For

16. Azad, I. W. F., p. 197.
17. Bandyopadhyay, *Jinnah*, p. 249.
18. Viccroy's letter to Jinnah, October 27 (S. I. N. C., II, p. cclxii).
19. Jinnah's letter to the Viccroy, October 27 (Ibid).
20. Liaqat Ali declared that under the Present Government of India there was no such thing as collective or joint responsibility. "There is no such thing as leadership of the

this entirely different approach of the League, Nehru remearked in his same note to Wavell, that in future, the position of the Congress "in the Cabinet will become increasingly difficult." He reminded Wavell that the Congress, on no account, was prepare "to function there as a group facing a rival group." And if this type of suspicions and direct conflict continued and the circumstances did not shape favourably, we may not find it possible to continue in the Government." Wavell's offer to the Deputy Chairmanship of the Cabinet Coordination Committee to Jinnah, was totally rejected by Nehru. Instead, he suggested to Wavell that a Cabinet Co-ordination Committee might be formed, apart from Wavell and Nehru, consisting of the Home member Sardar Ballabhbhai Patel, Industries and Supplies member Dr. John Mathai, Education Member C. Rajagopalachari, Finance member Liaqat Ali Khan and another representative of the League according to their choice.[21]

Suspicion and distrust continued in the mind of the nominees of the Muslim League. After the formation of Interim Government it was decided that all the members should meet informally before the formal meetings of the Cabinet, which would help to develop a convention that the Viceroy was only a constitutional head. Very often Nehru asked the members to tea through his private secretary. After the League joined the Interim Government, this practice of invitation continued as usual. Liaqat Ali took great objection to this and felt humiliated that a private secretary to Nehru should ask him to tea. Besides, he did not agree that Nehru as Vice-President of the Council could have right to hold such informal meetings. But Liaqat started holding similar meetings with the nominees of the League.[23] This was a small incident, but it showed how the members of the League created troubles in petty metters.

Government by one individual." S. W. J. N., Vol. I, p. 204 f.n.

21. Nehru's letter to Wavell, October 30 (S. W. J. N., Vol. I, pp. 203-205).

23. Azad, I. W. F., p. 180.

8

On the question of formation of the coalition ministries in the provinces, Wavell had an interview with Nehru and Liaqat, when same divergence of opinion crept up. On this question, Wavell remarked in his telegram to the Secretary of State : "Nehru suddenly blew up in characteristic fashion and denied the existence of a coalition in the centre since the Muslim League Members declined to recognise him as de facto Premier or to attend his daily cabinet meetings." But Liaqat remained calm and replied that "the Muslim League Members have every intention of co-operating in Central Cabinet and that League was quite prepared to discuss coalitions in provinces provided that it was general." But at the same time he "did not recognise Nehru as Premier and had come into work under existing Constitution." Wavell in his note remarked that the whole country was in a highly inflamable state and "we must be prepared for further trouble.[24]

For the constant opposition of the Muslim League, Nehru was greatly perturbed. In his letter to Krishna Menon,[25] Nehru expressed his great anxiety : "The Muslim League's gospel of hatred and preaching of violence has succeeded beyond their expectations......ever since the coming of the Muslim League, a very difficult situation has arisen and it faces us continually. These people are bent on mischief and give us a deal of trouble."[26]

Nehru's attitude of sending Krishna Menon on a tour of European countries without discussing the matter with the League, had been questioned by Wavell in his interview with Nehru in mid-November. On Viceroy's suspicion Nehru replied

---

24 Wavell's interview with Nehru and Liaqat, November 10, His telegram to the Secretary of State, November 11, 1946 (S. W. J. N., Vol. I, p. 206).

25. Krishna Menon was deputed as a personal representative of Nehru to visit some European countries to represent India's point of view.

26. Nehru's letter to V. K. Krishna Menon, November 11 (*Ibid*, p. 207).

that he was trying informally to "explore possibilities of developing diplomatic relations with various European Countries", and in case of good results in these informal approaches "action could have been decided upon on an official level. Krishna Menon seemed to me a very suitable person for this kind of work." Nehru believed that this type of action would not raise any communal activity. The Viceroy's advice to consult Liaqat beforehand, surprised Nehru. "I have told you previously", remarked Nehru in his letter to the Vieeroy, "that I find it difficult to function in the Government when some Ministers of the Government are not even agreeable to normal consultations and insist on keeping themselves apart as a block." Nehru even did not spare the Viceroy for his secret sympathy with the League and made a counter-charge by remarking : "It now appears not only that the Muslim League Members are giving to function as a separate block but that you wish to encourage them to do so. If any matter arises it is referred to Mr. Liaqat Ali Khan and me as if we represent to different blocs. And now you ask me to consult Mr. Liaqat Ali Khan in a matter which concerns my department and has absolutely nothing to do with him except in so far as he is one of the Members of Government. I am unable to accept this procedure."[27]

On November 14, Jinnah argued that the Interim Government was neither a Cabinet nor a Coalition but merely the Executive Council of the Governor-General. He again raised the cry for Pakistan by declaring in mid-November : "We shall resist anything that militates against the Pakistan demand", and accordingly instructed the League ministers to oppose any governmental action "which prejudiced this goal." He then denied the existence of a species called Indian and "pressed for an indefinite postponement of the Constituent Assembly."[28] On November 21, Jinnah went still further issuing a directive to the League that

27. Nehru's letter to the Viceroy, November 21 (*Ibid.*, pp. 213-215). Also N. Mansurg. *The Tranfer of Power* Vol. IX (London), pp. 122-124.

28. MBN, p. 324.

"no representative of the Muslim League will participate in the Constituent Assembly and the Bombay Resolution of the Muslim League Council passed on July 29 stands." Replying to Nehru's charge that the Muslim League was the "King's Party", Liaqat said : "If Pandit Nehru's discomfiture is due to the fact that the Muslim League bloc has refused to recognise the fiction of his leadership of the Government, then I can only sympathise with him."[29]

The atmosphere in the Interim Government grew so tense that the Congress members had twice threatened to resign. Thus out of utter disgust Nehru declared : "Over patience is fast reaching the limit ....If things continue on the same basis, a struggle on a large scale is inevitable." He became equally disgusted with the Viceroy for his failure to carry on the Interim Government in its original spirit by remarking : "Wavell is gradually removing the wheels of the car and this is leading to a critical situation." According to Nehru, ever since the Muslim League had joined the Government, it had tried utmost to enlist the British support. Earlier Nehru had written to Jinnah to settle their differences amicably without the Viceroy's intervention. But his advice had totally been ignored as "there is a mental alliance between the League and senior British Officials."[30]

At this time, Wavell tried to get on with the Constituent Assembly which should meet in the right atmosphere. But then the Muslim League was busy over the problem of Bihar[31] where communal disturbances broke out as a protest against the indiscriminate killings in East Bengal. The Viceroy had a talk with Jinnah, the latter advised strongly against calling the Constituent Assembly as he apprehanded to cause further communal trouble. On the other hand, Nehru pressed Wavell to call the Constituent Assembly immediately, pointing out that if it was

29. S. W. J. N., Vol. I, p. 216 f. n.
30. Dorothy, *Nehru*, II, pp. 273-274.
31. In a press conference at Karachi on November 26, Jinnah proposed the exchange of population for the interest of the minority community.

postponed now, there was no convenient date till April. Wavell thus decided to issue invitations hoping that before December9, the informal discussions between the Congress and the League might resume meanwhile. Accordingly on November 20, Wavell Invited the Constituent Assembly to meet on December 9. Jinnah sharply reacted to this and on the day following, he declared that no representative of the Muslim League would participate in the Constituent Assembly and reaffirmed the Bombay resolution of the League.[32]

Meanwhile the speeches of Jayaprakash Narayan alarmed Wavell so much that he called for Nehru's attention on this matter which might destroy the harmony between the two communities. Jayaprakash Narayan urged the people of U. P. to prepare for the impending struggle "which the country will have to lauch in near future to liquidate foreign imperialism." To win freedom, he called for a bigger revolution than that of 1942. But Nehru seemed to think it impossible that Jayaprakash Narayan could have said anything objectionable.[33]

As regards Congress decision to enter the Constituent Assembly, Nehru stated that if the League failed to accept the Cabinet Mission's proposals of May 16, there was no room for League's representatives in the Interim Government. Nehru believed that it was not the question whether the League joined it or not, but "We have accepted it and we shall get the fullest advantage out of it." About the advantage of the Constituent Assembly, Nehru said : "The only good thing about this Constituent Assembly is that...British power will not be directly represented in it." Nehru was firm in his determination that the Congress would go into this Assembly with full strength : "We will enter it, not in order to quarrel over petty things but to establish the Indian Repubilc."[34] On Nehru's insistence that the Viceroy's executive council could

32. S. W. J. N., vol. I, p. 238.
33. Wavell's record of interview with Nehru, November 19 (vide, *Ibid*).
34. I. A. R. vol. II, November 21, p. 279.

be termed a Cabinet, Jinnah exclaimed on November 25 : "Little things please little minds and you cannot turn a donkey into an elephant by calling it an elephant."[35] This verbal duelling revealed the crux of disagreement between Nehru and Jinnah.

London Conference, December 3-6

Ground began to slip from Wavell's feet for the firm determination of the British Government to transfer power without any further delay. The London authorities hinted to the Viceroy in unambiguous term not to appease anyone creating hindrance on the path of India's progress for freedom. So the Viceroy had no other option but to inform the Secretary of State on November 23, his failure to bring the League[36] in the Constituent Assembly.[37] At this point there seemed to be no way out of the current impasse; Attlee issued on invitation through the Viceroy to send two representatives of the Congress, two from the League and one from the Sikh to confer in London in an effort to reconcile. Nehru and the Congress Working Committee, sensing a trap were initially not in favour of accepting the invitation to attend the London Conference.[38] Any issue relating to the Constituent Assembly, the Congress believed, "should be settled and spaped by Indian hands on Indian soil for the Indian people", and it must be in India, not in London.

The Congress leaders and particularly Nehru thought that the British under the pressure from the League might revise or change the entire scheme of the Cabinet Mission's statement on May 16. Nehru gave vent to his feelings by writting a letter to the Viceroy on November 26 : "We have given careful thought to the proposal,...but we feel we cannot, at this stage, go to London ...The Muslim League accepted places in the Government

35. MBN, p. 325.
36. Wavell requested Liaqat Ali to act as a mediator to bring the League in the Constituent Assembly.
37. Bandopadhyay, *Jinnah*, p. 253.
38. MBN, p. 325, S. I. N. C., II, p. 811.

on the very clear understanding that they also accepted the long-term proposals contained in the Cabinet Mission's statement of May 16. Indeed they could not join the Government otherwise. But now, the League have announced very definitely that they will not participate in the Constituent Assembly. We attach, as you are aware, great importance to the holding of the meeting of of the Constituent Assembly on the date fixed, namely December 9. The invitation to us to go to London appears to us to reopen the whole problem which was settled to a large extent by the Cabinet Mission's statement and the formation of the Interim Government." Nehru insisted to hold the Constituent Assembly on the date fixed for it and any further postponement would result the abundonment of the whole plan. Any addition or change in the Constitutional scheme in London, was to wreck the whole scheme, making it difficult to replace it by another.[39]

In his cable to Attlee, Nehru informed him that the Congress had accepted the Cabinet Delegation's plan in its entirely. The Congress had no authority to change it as the leaders were committed to it. Hence his visit to London for this purpose was not necessary. But if necessary, it would be more suitable to visit London after the first brief session of the Constituent Assembly, when they would get more time for consultations. But inspite of this, "you wish to consider other matters you desire us to come, we shall endeavour to do so."[40] In reply Attlee assured Nehru that there was no intention of abandoning either the Constituent Assembly's decision or the plan advanced by the Cabinet Mission. It was the desire of the British Government to implement the plan in full. At the same time, Attlee also assured Jinnah that there was nothing in the plan to "prejudice full consideration of all points of view."[41]

The British Prime Minister invited Lord Wavell and the representatives of the Congress and the League to meet in London

39. Nehru's letter to Wavell, November 26 (Dorthy, *Nehru*, II pp. 275-276).
40. Nehru's cable to Attlee, November 28 (GIC, p. 659).
41. MBN, p. 325.

in another attempt to resolve the deadlock. When Nehru expressed his reluctance to go to London, Wavell persuaded Azad by arguing that "if the present attitude of the Muslim League continued, not only would the administration suffer but a peaceful solution of Indian problem would become more and more difficult." He further argued that discussions in London might take a more objective and dispassionate view as the leaders would be free from local pressure. Moreover Attlee had been a friend of India. These arguments convinced Azad who persuaded Nehru to attend the London Conference.[42] At last, Attlee's invitation to the Conference had been accepted. The Congress thought that the rejection of the London Conference might have given an opportunity to the British to change or withdraw the May 16th Cabinet Mission Plan. Nehru decided to participate in order not to "add to our enemies", or be accused in any way of rejecting the British plan to transfer power.[43] It was then decided that Nehru should go on behalf of the Congress. The League was represented by Jinnah and Liaqat Ali, while Baldev Singh went on behalf of the Sikhs.

Nehru reached London on December 3 and immediately after, he had an interview with Pethick-Lawrence. Nehru expressed his displeasure about commual riots and he believed that "the whole policy of Mr. Jinnah was antagonism, and the Muslim League depended on protest and disagreement". Nehru saw no hope of reconciliation with Jinnah and so it was useless to appease him, because "any gesture towards him merely encouraged violence in the country". Nehru had no hope of any good result from the proposed Conference and "he was somewhat disspirited" [44]

The London Conference was held at India Office at 10.30 A. M. Pethick-Laurence expressed about the British Government's anxiousness to transfer power to India smoothly, but in India,

42. Azad, I. W. F., p. 186.
43. MBN, pp. 327-328.
44. Nehru's interview with Pethick-Lawrence, London, December 3 (S.W.J.N., Vol. I, pp. 125-126).

the situation was not moving in that direction. The Cabinet Mission's suggestion of a three-tier system of government could only solve the situation. But "that co-operation seemed to be losing its hold on the thought of both parties". The Cabinet Mission objected the division of India and the only hope of solution rested on the grant of extended autonomy to the Muslim provinces on the lines proposed by the Mission. But the desired result was not obtained, replied Nehru. He held Muslim League responsible for non-cooperating in the government. He quoted the opinion of Jinnah, according to whom the Interim Government was not even a coalition, it was a government of two differing groups. The League conception of joining the government meant to stop other from functioning. The rank and file of the Muslim League were not interested in the three-tier system. "To them, coming in the Interim Government and the Constituent Assembly was a step in a conflict and not timely co-operation," stated Nehru in the Conference.

Asked by the Viceroy on the question of co-operation in the Interim Government, Nehru replied that the Muslim League members refused to meet him. The Viceroy then pointed out to Nehru that it was Nehru who had declined to meet Liaqat Ali, at least on two occasions, when Liaqat sought co-operation from him. To this question Nehru promptly replied that Liaqat insulted him and there was no reason to meet Liaqat at that time.[45] On the very first day of the Interim Government, Nehru had been insulted and almost assaulted by the Muslims outside the Viceroy's House. Even recently two Muslim representatives, M. A. H. Ispahani and Begum Shah Nawaz, had gone to the United States and had made virulent speches at the *New York Herald* forum.[46]

45. Muslim League members carrying black flag and shouting slogans staged the demonstration outside Viceroy's House on the first day of the Interim Government.

46. In a debate on Indian affairs Ispahani declared: "The League's participation in the Interim Government means... that the struggle for Pakistan will now be carried on within as well as outside the Government."

Stafford Cripps said that the League joined in the government on another interpretation and in fact that was intended by the Cabinet Mission. Under the present Nehru government, the provinces had been given an option to come out of the group; but the original principle was that the provinces should see the whole picture of the group constitution "before deciding whether to go in or stay out." "On the Congress interpretation", Cripps argued "the Muslims quite rightly feel that are deprived of the opportunity of making a complete picture of the group constitution." Wavell also supported Cripps by saying' that the "intension of the Mission was that the sections should frame provincial constitution." Nehru completely disagreed with these arguments and said that it was "an impossible position for the Congress to accept or tolerate for a moment that the provincial constitutions should be framed by the majority vote of the section, which might be composed entirely of persons from other provinces." Nehru was opposed on the question of compulsory grouping of the provinces.[47] In his letter to Vijayalakshmi Pandit, Nehru wrote that the Muslim League "want some kind of compulsory grouping and the British Government say that to some extent the Muslim League's interpretation of their statement is justified." But the Congress were of opinion that there should be no compulsory grouping of the provinces., "the provinces should vote as a unit in the sections." About the communal riots in India, he held the League resposible for it. "This habit of stabbing which the Muslim League has started and encouraged is likely to continue," Nehru wrote to Mrs. Pandit, holding Viceroy responsible for such actions. The Viceroy had been "functioning in complete accordance with the Muslim League and this has encouraged their troublesome and violent activities."[48]

On December 6 Strafford Cripps asked Nehru to make an agreement with the League, but Nehru did not think any real

47. Minutes of the London Conference, (S. W. J. N., Vol. pp. 127-132).
48. Nehru's letter to Vijayalakshmi Pandit, London, December 5, (J. N. Papers).

agreement was possible under that circumstance. When asked by Pethic-Lawrence how the Constituent Assembly would go at its opening session, Nehru replied that they would set up various Committees. The Advisory Committee would consist of three sections, Tribal Areas, Fundamental Rights and Minorities Some places would be left for Muslim League, if the League wanted to join. But there must be a good start. In case of difference of opinion between the Congress and the League, Nehru said that the matter could be referred to the Federal Court for decision. Jinnah then intervened and asked about the position when "the Federal Court took a different view of the interpretation of the document from that held by H M. G."[49] and in that case, the decision of the Federal Court would not be binding on the League. Jinnah further observed : "that the Constituent Assembly would decide by a large Hindu majority to refer the matter to the Federal Court and would be bound by Federl Court's ruling. The Muslim League could not, therefore, be a party to such a reference as they were not prepared to be bound by it."[50]

Attlee made three comments on Nehru's arguments. Firstly, the British Prime Minister "could not admit that any addition had been made to the statement of May 16th. Secondly, the present statement could not be termed pressure from outside on the Constituent Assembly and thirdly, he could not agree that there was any short of disagreement on the Constituent Assembly except that of working within an agreed framework."[51] From the proceedings of the London Conference, it became clear that Jinnah got sufficient encouragement to carry on his plan of Pakistan.

After the end of the Conference, the following statement had been issued on December 6 :

"The conversation held by His Majesty's Government with Pandit Jawaharlal Nehru, Mr. M. A. Jinnah, Mr. Liaqat Ali Khan

---

49. His Majesty's Government.
50. Minutes of the London Conference, December 6 (*Ibid*).
51. *Ibid*.

and Sardar Baldev Singh came to an end this evening as Pandit Nehru and Sardar Baldev Singh are returning to India tomorrow morning.

"The object of the Conversations has been to obtain the participation and co-operation of all parties in the Constituent Assembly. It is not expected that any final settlement could be arrived at, since the Indian representatives must consult their colleagues before any final decision is reached.

"The Cabinet Mission have throughout maintained the view that the decisions of the sections should, in the absence of an agreement to the contrary, be taken by a simple majority vote of the representatives in the sections. This view has been accepted by the Muslim League but the Congress have put forward a different view. They have asserted that the true meaning of the statement, read as a whole, is that the provinces have the right to decide both as to grouping and as to their own constitution.

"On the matter immediately in dispute, His Majesty's Government urge the Congress to accept the view of the Cabinet Mission in order that a way may be opened for the Muslim League to reconsider their attitude.

"There has never been any prospect of success for the Constituent Assembly except upon the basis of the agreed procedure. Should a constitution come to be framed by the Constituent Assembly in which a large section of the Indian population has not been represented, His Majesty's Government could not of course, contemplate as the Congress have stated they would not contemplate forcing such a constitution upon any unwilling parts of the country."[52] The above statement of the British Cabinet was a clear indication of its open support to the Muslim League.

---

52. British Cabinet's statement, December 6 (S. I. N. C., II, pp. 811-12).

At the time of his departure from London, Nehru met the Press and expressed hope about the self determining status of the Constituent Assembly by observing: "The Constituent Assembly will be a self-governing and self-determining body which will not tolerate any outside interference. Regarding British newspapers one gets the wrong impression that there is an impending tragedy in India which is to be averted by bringing us to London for a magical settlement. The situation in India is in many respects distressing but there is nothing to get excited about. ...The question of success or failfure of the talks has no meaning. The major thing is that the Constituent Assembly will be meeting in three days time."[53] After making this statement in London, Nehru returned to India hurridly to take part in the first meeting of the Constituent Assembly scheduled to be held on December 9.

Jinnah and Liaqat did not return to India immediately but remained in London. They utilised the opportunity and became successful in enlisting their support from the leading statesmen of Britain. Jinnah advocated that there was no time in fruitless discussion with the Congress, but the League's only mission to establish Pakistan for the Muslim. During his stay in London Jinnah got the wholehearted support from the Conservative Party of Britain. On December 13, Churchill, the leader of the opposition in Parliament remarked that under Nehru's four months Interim Government, so many people lost their lives or wounded, which baffled all calculation of death within a period of last ninety years. The Muslim minorities mainly became the prey of assassination. The attempt for establishing Hindu majority rule in India could be frustrated only by a civil war.[54] These uttar-

53. Nehru's address to Indian Press Correspondents, London, December 6 (S. W. J. N., Vol. I, p. 140).

54. Woolput, Stenley, *Jinnah of Pakistan* (New York, 1984), pp. 303-304 Churchill had a secret correspondence with Jinnah. Such a "Personal and Confidential" letter of Churchill dated August 3, 1946 had been published in *Hindustan Times*, Delhi, on June 16, 1987.

ances of Churchill inspired Jinnah with a new vigour. Jinnah also got the support of a number of responsible British officials in London, from whom he came to know that if the Congress did not accept the Cabinet Mission Plan in its entirety, the British Government would be forced reluctantly to divide India [55]

London Conference made Jinnah popular among a large section of British officials, while Nehru-Congress became isolated from them.

55. Bandopadhyay, *Jinnah*, p. 256.

CHAPTER—VII

DECISION FOR INDIA'S PARTITION

Nehru hurriedly returned from England to give shape of his cherished dream—the Constitution of free India. The first meeting of the Constituent Assembly was held on December9, while Jinnah from England, urged Wavell repeatedly to postpone the Constituent Assembly meeting *sine die*. But Nehru carried out his point firmly caring little for Jinnah's opposition. On the question of electing the President of the Assembly, Nehru and Patel were of view that someone should be elected President who was not in the government. After several discourses, Rajendra Prasad was elected President, though he was a member of the government.[1]

On December 13, Nehru made his momentous speech, pointing out the aims and objectives of the Constituent Assembly by observing : "For a long time we have been having various plans for a free India in our minds, but now, when we are beginning the actual work, I hope, you will be at one with me when I say, that we should present a clear picture of this plan to ourselves, to the people of India and to the world at large. The resolution that I am placing before you defines our aims, describes an outline of the plan and points the way which we are going to trend."[2] The resolution that Nehru placed before the meeting was in the nature of a pledge, drafted after mature consideration with a view to avoid controversy. Nehru described this resolution as "an understanding with ourselves and with the millions of our brothers and sisters who live in this great country." Accordingly Nehru moved the following resolutions :

"1. This Constituent Assembly declares its firm and solemn resolved to proclaim India as an Independent Sovereign Republic and to draw up for her future goverance a Constitution;

---

1. Azad, I. W. F., p. 187.
2. S. W. J. N., Vol. I, pp. 240-241.

2. Wherein the territories that now comprise British India, the territories that now form the Indian States as well as such other territories as are willing to be constituted into the Independent Soverign India, shall be a Union of them all ; and

3. Wherein the said territories, whether with their present boundaries or with such others as may be determined by the Constituent Assembly and thereafter according to the Law of tho Constitution, shall possess and retain the status of autonomous Units, together with residuary powers, and exercise all powers and functions of government and administration, save and except such powers and functions as are vested in or assigned to the Union, or as are inherent or implied in the Union or resulting therefrom; and

4. Wherein all power and authority of the Sovereign Independent India, its constituent parts and organs of government, are derived from the people, and

5. Wherein shall be guaranteed and secured to all the people of India justice, social, economic and political, equality of status, of opportunity, and before the law; freedom of thought, expression, belief, faith, worship, vocation, association and action, subject to law and public morality; and

6. Wherein adequate safeguards shall be provided for minorities, backward and tribal areas, and depressed and other backward classes; and

7. Wherein shall be maintained the integrity of the territory of the Republic and its Sovereign rights on land, sea and air according to justice and law of civilised nations; and

8. This ancient land attain its rightful and honoured place in the world and make its full and willing contribution to the promotion of world peace and the welfare of mankind".[3]

---

3. Quoted in *Ibid,* pp 243-244; Dorothy, *Nehru* II, 278-279.

According to Nehru, it was not merely a resolution but a declaration and a firm resolve. It was a pledge and undertaking for all Indians. He belived it the right time "when we should, so for as we are capable of it, rise above our ordinary selves and party disputes and think of the great problem before us in the widest and most tolerant and most effective manner so rhat, whatever we may produce, should be worthy a whole". On this auspicious day, Nehru did not forget the moving spirit behind this and paid his respect to that great leader. "There is another person who is absent here", remarked Nehru with due respect, "who must be in the minds of many of us today—the great leader of our people, the father of our nation—who has been the architect of this Assembly and all that has gone before it and possibly of much that will follow. He is not here because, in pursuit of his ideals, he is ceaselessly working in a far corner of India.[4] But I have no doubt that his spirit hovers over this place and blesses our undertaking".[5]

On the eve of making a Constitution for India, Nehru believed that "India is going to have a powerful effect on the rest of the world" and she after independence "immediately play an important and a vital part in world affairs. Even on the verge of freedom, India had begun to play a prominent part in world affairs[6]. In world affairs, India wanted to make friends even with England, inspite of her long history of conflict in the past. "The only way to influence india is through friendship and co-operation and good- will", continued Nehru in his speech, remarking "We have to work together in this country and we have inevitably to co-operate, if not to-day, tomorrow or the day after". So India must try for co-operation "in the largest measure". But at the same time, he clarified his idea of co-operation. "Co-operation cannot mean the giving up of the fundamental ideals on which we have stood and on which we should stand. It is not co-operation

4. Gandhiji was then travelling through the disturbed areas in the interior of Noakhali district.

5. S. W. J. N., Vol. I, p. 245.

6. In the Interim Government, Nehru extended support to the Indonesian freedom struggle. In December 1946, Vijayalakshmi Pandit, leader of Indian delegation, urged to U. N. O. for ending the France regime in Spain.

to surrender everything that has given meaning to our lives". The constitution building had a great task for the people of India. "In this Constituent Assembly", Nehru remarked "We are functioning on a world stage and the eyes of the world are upon us and the eyes of our entire past are upon us"[7]. In reply to Churchill's statement that England would not be bound by decisions of the Constituent Assembly of India, Nehru stated, "whatever form of constitution we may decide upon in the Constituent Assembly will become the Constritution of free India—whether Britain accepts it or not". He further gave vent to his emotion by stating: "We have now stopped looking towards London", reminding Churchill that the Indians "will not tolerate any outside interference".[8]

Two days after on December 15, Nehru came to Varanasi where he led stress about the importance of the Constituent Assembly. About Churchill's remark, Nehru's mind was still bitter and so again he clarified India's stand with Britain by observing : "India's relations with Britain henceforth will depend on how the British act at present. We want to be friendly with all countries of the world, even with Britain, but only if Britain does not put hindrances in our march towards complete freedom. We want to forget British misdeeds of the past. If the British behaviour towards India at present improves, Britain would reap favourable results, but if Britain's behaviour towards India does not change she cannat expect good result".[9] About the possibility of India's partition and Hindu-Muslim relation, Nehru stated : "Pakistan is not the right solution of the communal problem. Even If the country were divided, crores of Hindus and Muslims would continue to live in Pakistan and Hindustan without any rights of citizenship and the commual problem would remain still unsolved. The idea of exchange of populatian on such a vast scale is absolutely ridicluous".[10]

Nehru also wanted the Princely States to participate in the Constitution making proceedure, as it was a matter of whole of

7. Dorothy, *Nehru*, II, pp. 286-287.
8. MBN, p. 330.
9. The Hindustan Times 17. 1946.
10. S. W. J. N., Vol. I, p. 252.

India. Accordingly on December 21, a Constituent Assembly Negotiating Committee was formed, consisting of Nehru, Patel, Azad, Sitaramayya, Shankarrao Deo and N. Gopalaswami Ayyangar to confer with the Negotiating Committee of the Princes Chamber on the distribution and the method of election of the Constituent Assembly of 93 representatives of the Indian States.[11]

After the London Conference, the tone of the British government became definitely in favour of the Muslim League. On the question of the Constituent Assembly and the Federal Court, Pethick-Lawrence stated in the House of Lords on December 17 : "I should make it quite plain that the British Government do not consider that this issue is one which is to be desirable to refer to the Federal Court. The Statement of December 6th makes this clear and also the interpretation which the British Government themselves hold." This statement alarmed the Congress as because to accept the document of December 6 was to give highest moral victory to the League.[12] Therefore, the Congress Working Committee on its meeting held on December 22, gave a careful consideration of the statement issued by the British Government, which seemed to them a clear departure of the Cabinet Mission's statement of May 16, resolved : "Inspite of this explicit statement the British Government have on December 6, issued a statement which is both an addition to, and an interpretation of the Statement of May 16, 1946. They have done so after more than six and a half months, during which period many developments have taken place as a consequence of the original statement.

"Throughout this period the position of the Congress was made repeatedly clear to the British Government or their representatives, and it was with full knowledge of this position that the British Government took subsequent steps in furtherance of the Cabinet Mission's proposals. That position was in conformity with the basic principles laid down in the Statement of May 16, 1946, which statement the Congress had accepted in its entirety.

"Further, the Congress had expressed its willingness to refer, if necessity arose, the point of interpretation to the Federal

11. *Ibid*, p. 256.
12. S. I. N. C., Vol. II, p. 815.

Court, whose decision should be accepted by the parties concerned. In the course of his letter dated June 28, 1946, addressed to Mr. Jinnah, the Viceroy stated that the Congress had accepted the Statement of May 16. In the course of a broadcast on August 24, 1946, the Viceroy in appealing to the Muslim League to co operate, pointed out that the Congress is ready to agree that any dispute of interpretation may be referred to the Federal Court.

"The Muslim League reversed its former decision and rejected the British Cabinet Mission's scheme by formal resolution and even decided to resort to 'direct action'. Their spokesmen have since repeatedly challenged the very basis of that scheme, that is, the constitution of a Union of India and have reverted to their demand for a partition of India. Even after the British Government statement of December 6, 1946, the leaders of the Muslim League have reiterated this demand for partition and the establishment of two separate independent governments in India.

"Inspite of this assurance and of previous assurances to the effect that no additions to, or interpretations of the Statement of May 16, 1946, were going to be made, the British Government have now issued a statement which clearly, in several respects, goes beyond the original statement, on the basis of which progress has been made till now.

"The Congress seeks to frame, through the Constituent Assembly, a constitution of a free and independent India with the willing co-operation of all elements of the Indian people. The Working Committee regret that the Muslim League members of the Constituent Assembly have refrained from attending its opening session.

"In this statement of December 6, 1946, the British Government in giving their interpretation of a doubtful point of procedure have referred to it as a 'fundamental point' and suggested that the Constituent Assembly may refer it to the Federal Court at the very early date. Subsequent statements made on behalf of the British Government have made it clear that they are not prepared to accept the decision of this court should it go against their own interpretation. On behalf of the Muslim League also it has been stated they will not be bound by the decision of the Federal Court and a demand for partition of India, which is a negation of the Cabinet Mission's scheme continues to be put forward.

"The Working Committee are still of opinion that the interpretation put by the British Government in regard to the method of voting in the sections is not in conformity with provincial autonomy, which is one of the fundamental basis of the scheme proposed in the statment of May 16. The Committee are auxious to avoid anything that may come in the way of successful working of the Constituent Assembly and are prepared to do everything in their power to seek and obtain the largest measure of co-operation provided that no fundamental principle is violated".[13]

The Muslim League's success in harrassing the Congress from its joining in the Interim Government in October 1946 to March 1947 was greatly due to the part played by Wavell in India's struggle for freedom. Wavell deliberately ignored Nehru's persistent demand that the League as it did not accept the Cabinet Mission Plan of May 1946, be dismissed from the Interim Government. After the London Conference, while Wavell was still in London, Patel privately wrote Cripps on December 15, accusing Wavell his secret sympathy towards the League. "The Viceroy here took the contrary view, and every action of his since the Great Calcutta Killing has been in the direction of encouragement to the Muslim League and putting pressure on us towards appeasement".[14] Nehru also during his brief stay in London made it clear before the ministers about Wavell's partiality towards the League. Wavell's attitude and his unpopularity among a large sectian of Indian people might have told heavily on Attlee's mind, who decided to replace the Viceroy.

There was still no agreement about framing of the new Constitulion. When the League joined the Interim Government in October, Jinnah told Wavell that the League was ready to accept the Cabinet Miccion's constitutional plan, provided the Congress would accept the plan unequivocally. The Viceroy as

13. Resolution of the Congress Working Committee, December 22, S. I. N. C., Vol. II. pp. 816-819.

14. Letter from Patel to Cripps, December 15 (Patel's Correspondance, Vol. 3, pp. 313-315).

well as the British government tried hard ro extract from the Congress an acceptance of the intended plan of the Cabinet Mission rather than Congress's own interpretation, and in January 1947, the All India Congress Committee came near a genuine acceptance of the plan. But they still insisted some qualifications advocating that no province or part of a province could be compelled against its wishes to remain in a particular group. While this controversy was still in progress, Gandhiji, who was then in East Bengal, openly advised the Assam Congress Committee not to go into their section as provided in the plan.[15]

1947 was the most eventful year for the Congress as well as for the country. On January 5, the All India Congress Committee held its meeting in New Delhi to consider the statement of December 6 by the British Cabinet about its acceptance or rejection. The meeting took place in the hall of the Constitution Club where Assam Congress leaders figured prominently in the discussions. They attended the meeting to safeguard their own interest and wanted to see the implementation of the pledges made by the 'Congress High Command' that Assam would not be forced into the C section. But if they were forced, they considered it a breach of understanding. The Assam leaders believed that the last paragraph of December 6 statement might not save them, for it was primarily meant for Muslims. The words in the statement were as under: "Should the constitution come to be framed by a Constituent Assembly in which a large section of the Indian population has not been represented, His Majesty's Government could not of course contemplate forcing such a constitution upon any unwilling parts of the country".

The A. I. C. C. now began tn discuss whether the December 6 statement was to be accepted. If it was rejected then it would mean that the Congress had put itself out of the pale of the statement of May 16 as interpreted by the statement of December 6 and therefore could not afford a change for the Muslim League to join the Constituent Assembly. It would encourage the League to formulate a Centre for them and would therefore ask for a new writ from Britain which they might obtain in view of the latter's sympathy with the League. The old writ in favour of a common

15. Moon, *Gandhi*, p. 254

centre mihgt not run on the ground that the Congress had not accepted the statement of December 6. Accordingly a new writ was necessary to meet the situation created by the new attitude of the Congress. The British thus would have a good opportunity of departing from their earlier statement of May 16 for a common centre. This would create inevitably for two centres of Pakistan and Hindustan, supporting the very basis of two nation theory.[16]

On the other hand, the Congress believed that if the statement was accepted, it was to create equally great dangers. It was to rise the prestige of Jinnah to the highest hight, who might dictate more terms, even like the group armies in India. The League might ask for fifty percent in the service of the army and in the legistature. Under these conditions, the A. I. C. C. accepted the suggestion of the Working Committee, for the time being.

After considering the events that had taken place in the country, the A. I. C. C. undertook the following main resolutions :

"While the Congress has always been agreeable to making a reference to the Federal Court on the question of interpretation in dispute, such a reference has become purposeless and undesirable owing to recent announcements made on behalf of the British Government...... .

"The A. I. C. C. is firmly of opinion that the constitution for a free and independent India should be framed by the people of India on the basis of as wide an agreement as possible....... The A. I. C. C. realises and appreciates the difficulties placed in the way of some provinces, notably Assam, Baluchistan and N. W. F. P. and the Sikhs in the Punjab, by the British Cabinet scheme of May 16, 1946, and more especially by the interpretation put upon it by the British Government in their statement of December 6, 1946. The Congress cannot be a party to any such compulsion or imposition against the will of the people concerned, a principle which the British Government have themselves recognised.

"The A. I. C. C. is anxious that the Constituent Assembly should proceed with the work of framing the constitution for free India with the goodwill of all parties concerned and, with a view to removing the difficulties that have arisen owing varying inter-

16. S. I. N. C., II, pp. 820-821.

pretations, agree to advise action in accordance with the interpretation of the British Government in regard to the procedure tc be followed in the sections. It must be clearly understood, however, that this must not involve any compulsion of a province and that the rights of the Sikhs in the Punjab should not be jeopordised. In the event of any attempt at such compulsion, a province or part of a province has the right to take such action as may be deemed necessary in order to give effect to the wishes of the people concerned...."[17]

The resolution of the Congress thus accepted the compulsory grouping of the provinces, but at the same time it left scope for Assam to join in a particular group according to its wish. There was ample time for Assam to decide for itself what it should do. The A. I. C. C. thus did not want to purchase peace at the cost of Assam. This resolution of the Congress did not satisfy the League but at the same time, the resolution created indirect acceptance of India's partition.[18]

The League's participation in the Constituent Assembly became a distant cry, creating the situation difficult and delicate. The League at first accepted and then rejected the Cabinet Mission Plan. The league boycotted the Constituent Assembly though it was in session. The people became impatient for the attainment of freedom, while there was no solution of communal problem.

The League met at Karachi on January 29 and resolved not to participate in the deliberations of the Constituent Assembly. The League characterised the A. I. C. C.'s resolution of January 6 "as no more than a dishonest trick, a piece of verbal jugglery intended to decive the British Government, the Muslim League and Public opinion." It criticised the Congress resolutions which went beyond the scope permitted by the Cabinet Mission's statement of May 16 and urged His Majesty's Government in London to declare the failure of the Cabinet Mission Plan. But some

17. Quoted in *Ibid,* p. 822.

18. V. P. Menon, the most trustworthy of Patel mentioned that the later had already formulated plan for India's partition. Meanwhile some top ranking Congress leaders also began to think partition inevitable.—MTP, pp. 358-359.

impartial observers from London asserted that the plan had not been failed, commenting that "the Constituent Assembly was neither a party caucus nor exclusively Hindu, as non-Muslim minorities were well-represented."[19] But the League was not disturbed by such comments and went one step further demanding to declare the meetings of the Constituent Assembly invalid. On the other hand, in Congress's view, the League's resolution constituted its non-acceptance of the May 16 statement. Accordingly on February 5, Nehru firmly asked Wavell to dismiss the League's members from the government, but the Viceroy took no action.[20]

The British government, dispairing of bringing the parties to agreement now took a bold decision. Attlee—the British Prime Minister, announced on February 20 that it was His Majesty's definite intention to transfer power to responsible Indian hands by a date not later than June 1948.[21] The text of his announcement was as under :

"It has long been the policy of successive British Government to work towards the realisation of self government in India. In pursuance of this policy an increasing measure of responsibility has been devolved on Indians, and today the civil administration and the Indian armed forces rely to a very large extent on Indian civilians and officers...In 1940, the Coalition Government recognised the principle that Indians should themselves frame a new constitution for a fully autonomus India, and in the offor of 1942 they invited them to set up a Constituent Assembly for this purpose as soon as the war was over.

"The British Government believe this policy to have been right and the Cabinet Mission sent to India last year spent over three months in consultation with Indian leaders in order to help them to agree udon a method for determining the future constitution of India, so that the transfer of power might be smoothly and rapidly effected. It was only when it seemed clear that without some initiative from the Cabinet Mission, agreement was unlikely to be reached that they put forward proposals themselves.

19. S. I. N. C., II, p. 823.
20. Nehru's letter to Wavell, February 5, 1947 (Prasad's papers).
21. S. I. N. C., II, p. 823, Azad, I. W. F., p. 190.

"It is with great regret that His Majesty's Government find that there are st:ll differences among Indian parties which are preventing the Constituent Assembly from functioning as it was intended that it should.

"His Majesty's Government desire to hand over the responsibility to authorities established by a constitution approved by all parties in India in accordance with the Cabinet Mission's Plan, but unfortunately there is at present no clear prospect that such a constitufion and such authorities will emerge. The present state of uncertainty is fraught with danger and cannot be indefinitely prolonged. His Majesty's Government wish to make it clear that it is their definite intention to take necessary steps to effect the transference of power to responsible Indian hands by a date not later than June, 1948.

"It is therefore essential that all parties should sink their differences in order that thay may be ready to shoulder the great responsibilities which will come upon them next year".[22]

The Prime Minister, at the same time, made it clear that lack of agreement would not cause the postponement of the date. If within the specified date, no constitution had been agreed upon, the British Government would have to consider "to whom the powers of the Central Government in British India should be handed over, on the due date, whether as a whole to some form of Central Government, or in such other way as may seem most reasonable and in the best interests of the Indian people".[23]

In his announcement, the Prime Minister extended his co-operation and good-will to the Indian people : "The British Government cannot conclude this statement without expressing on behalf of people of this country their good-will and good-wishes towards the people of India as they go forward to this final stage in their achievement of self-government. It will be the wish of everyone in these islands that, notwithstanding constitutional changes, the association of the British and Indian peoples should not be brought to an end; and they will wish to continue to do all that is in their power to further the well-being of India".[24]

22. Quoted in S. I. N. C., II, pp. 823-824.
28. Ibid, p. 825; Moon, *Gandhi*, p. 254.
24. *Ibid.*

The appointment of Wavell as the Viceroy was also terminated and in his place, the name of Mountbatten had been declared to suceed him, who was entrusted with the task af transferring to Indian hands responsibility for the government of British India "that will ensure the future happiness and prosperity of India". Thus Wavell was relieved of his charge, who did not tender his resignation by choice. But he continued his office till March 22 when Mountbatten arrived and relieved him.[25]

Wavell did not agree about the announcement of a particular date of India's freedom. He wished to persist with the Cabinet Mission Plan. He held the view that the British government would fail in its duty if it tranferred power before the solution of India's communal problem. Withdrawl of British power in such a tense situation would lead to widespread riots and disturbances. He, therefore, advised to maintain the status-quo till the differences of two major parties were settled. But he could not convince Attlee for latter's firm coviction of India's freedom.[26]

The announcement of Attlee to trasfer power in the hands of Indian leaders within the specified time-limit, encouraged the Congress leaders to proceed with "an accelerated speed". They cared little about the various implications in the announcement. But Gandhiji held a different view. To him, the transfer of power was not a problem of power politics but a just and moral solution. He wanted the majorities to work for meeting the anxieties of the minorities, and was not prepared for partition. He advised the Congress "not to accept any arrangement in a hurry, which they might have to repent at leisure" and wanted the Congressmen to be prepared for worse circumstance, instead of India's partition. But his advice did not bear fruits before the Congress leaders, who like the British, judged the situation in terms of political necessity. The Congress leaders feared that delay or vacillation might drift the country to a civil war.[27]

Actually the whole of northern India, from Bihar to Peshawar was in a state of communal war. The bloodshed, arson, loot and

25. *Ibid.*, p. 826.
26. Azad, I. W. F., p. 190.
27. NMG, p. 489.

rapacity continued unabated in which thousands of non-Muslims lost their lives. The league volunteers work better assured than their opponents. Meanwhile on March 6, Churchill's statement in the British parliament added fuel to the fire when he criticised the mistaken policy of the British government to allow Nehru to form the Interim Government as a leader of the caste Hindus. According to him, there was no time to implement the Cripps Proposal of 1942, but now the partition of India was the logical conclusion.[28]

During this period of high tension, Nehru and Patel had taken upon themselves the sole responsibilites for making political decisions, It was in the absence of Gandhiji and without any prior consultation with him that the Working Committee of the Congress made its epoch-making decisions between March 6 and 8. It affirmed that the Indian constitution would apply only to those areas which accepted it. It also made it clear that any province or part of a province which accepted the constitution and desired to join in the Indian Union could do so according to their will. It left no illusion in the mind of Jinnah about the creation of Pakistan—his cherished dream. The Working Committee of the Congress proposed the partition of the Punjab into two provinces, its western part would belong to the Muslim, while lhe eastern, to the Hindu-Sikhs. About Bengal, the Congress did not propose for its partition, but it was clear by implication that the Congress would rather demand a similar partition of Bengal than let the whole province be formed within Pakistan. Nehru had to accept this position in view of League's continual harrassment, realising that there was no prospect of an agreement with the League. The only alternative to the Cabinet Mission Plan, which Nehru thought was the best solution of Indian problem, was the partition of the Punjab and Bengal.[29]

The official announcement of the Congress about the partition of the Punjab obviously led to the recognition of the partition of

28. Moon, Penderel, *Divide and Quit*. (London, 1964), p388.
29. W. V. J., pp. 426-427. The Congress leadership still believed that Jinnah would never accept the partition of Bengal and the Punjab. He would not be satisfied with only a truncated Pakistan.

the country. The demand for Pakistan was indirectly recognised. Jinnah became greatly rejoiced and told before the Muslim Press at Bombay on March 12 that the ideals, aims and basic principles of the Muslims were not only different from the Hindus, but were opposites to the extreme. There was a time, when the people laughed at the creation of Pakistan but now the Muslims were going to have their own land with honour.[30]

During this time Gandhiji came to Patna from Noakhali touring the riot-afflicted areas of Bihar and collecting money from the Hindus for the relief of the Muslim sufferers. He could not understand fully the implications of Attlee's announcement of February 20, neither he was in any touch with the latest development in Delhi. When therefore he read in the newspaper that on March 8, the Congress Working Committee had passed a resolution proposing the division of the Punjab, he was greatly perturbed. He rightly understood the resolution as a prelude to the acceptance of partition. He immediately wrote to Nehru and Patel expressing his inability to understand the resolution and asking them to explain It. Patel replied that it had been adopted after the deepest deliberation, but if Gandhiji disagreed, he might say what he felt to be right. Nehru replied that the partition was a necessity, "so that reality might be brought into the picture". He further said that this was the only answer to partition as demanded by Jinnah.[31]

Before the transfer of power, an important step had been taken by the leaders of Bengal for the creation of "a sovereign Bengal", that would neither join with the Indian Union nor with Pakistan. The leaders of this movement were Suhrawardy and Sarat Chandra Bose. The leaders of the Bengal Muslim League, Suhrawardy and Nazimuddin had been dissatisfied for the nomination of Jogendra Nath Mandal from Bengal. In this movement, Suhrawardy was greatly assisted by Abdul Hashim, the secretary of the Bengal Muslim League. From January 1947, these Muslim

30. Woolpert, p. 312.
31. Moon, *Gandhi*, pp. 255-256. The Working Committee resolution had been prompted by the serious communal riots in the Punjab from March 4 which continued for a fortnight. The province seemed ready for further communal riots.

leaders met several times with Sarat Chandra Bose, the local leader of Bengal Congress, and prepared the draft proposal of an independent Bengal. The main idea underlying this scheme was to resist the partition of Bengal for creating an independent state. They tried to pursue this scheme with courage as because after the British government's statement on February 20, Shyama Prasad Mukherjee, the leader of the Hindu Mahasabha, began to make forceful demand for the partition of Bengal.[32]

According to their plan, Bengal was to be divided, for administrative purposes, into three units—West, Central and East. The territory of "Greater Bengal" would extend from Purnea to Assam. The Central Bengal was to consist of all Muslim majority districts, like the district of Chittagong Division, Dacca Division, the Presidency Division, Rajshahi Division and the district of Sylhet. The rest of Assam would form as the Eastern Zone, while the districts of Burdwan Division and Purnea would form Western Zone of the province. In the Bengal Assembly there would be the system of equal representations of both the communities. The office of the head of the state would rotate among the Hindus, Muslims and other minor communities. The experiment would continue for a period of ten years only and if it could not properly work, the three units of the Greater Bengal would have the right to join either with India or with Pakistan.[33]

The outline of this sovereign Bengal Plan was forwarded to Gandhiji by Sarat Chandra Bose and to Jinnah by Suhrawardy under the following three main clauses :

1. The Muslim League government of Bengal would continue to hold office and some new nominees of the Bengal Congress were to be appointed immediately.
2. Bengal would neither join with Hindustan or Pakistan but to remain united and free. The fate of Bengal would be decided by Bengal Constituent Assembly, which was to be elected on universal adult franchise.
3. The seats for the Hindus, the Muslims, the scheduled castes and other minorities were to be fixed according to their population ratios.[34]

---

32. Bandopadhyay, *Jinnah*, p. 278.
33. Kamaruddin, *East Pakistan*, pp. 88-89.

The reaction of this plan was immediate and mostly adverse among both the communities. Besides the Hindu Mahasabha, the partition of Bengal was demanded by almost all the Congress leaders except Sarat Chandra Bose and Kiron Shanker Roy. Jinnah strongly condemned the move of partitioning the province, but wanted to see whole of Bengal within Pakistan. Nehru was against the decision of an independent Bengal and did not like much on important issue to be discussed in the Provincial level disregarding the views of the Congress high command. He feared that this proposal would involve the whole of Bengal within Pakistan in due course of time. Moreover, the Bengal Congress, at no stage, involved itself officially with this plan of sovereign Bengal. Hence the plan of Suhrawardy and Sarat Chandra Bose was abandoned by both the Congress and the League.[35]

By the middle of March, partition of Bengal became an accomplished fact. Acharya Kripalani the Congress President, raised his voice for the partition of Bengal while Gandhiji remarked that If Bengal was partitioned he communal problem in eastern India would become a permanent feature.[36] Wavell also at the time of his departure from India said that if communal difficulties led to violence, history would not forgive the British.

About the hasty decision of the Congress due to Attlee's statement on February 20, Azad remarked : "It is difficult to say which of the two alternatives—the one actually adopted by Mr. Attlee or the one suggested by Mr. Wavell—would have been better for India. If Lord Wavell's advice had been followed and the solution of the Indian problem deferred for a year or two, it is possible that the Muslim League would have got tired of opposition......It is possible that perhaps the tragedy of Indian partition may have been avoided. One cannot say for certain but a year or two is nothing in the history of a nation."[37]

---

34. *Ibid*, p. 89.
35. Sen, Shila, *Muslim Politics in Bengal, 1937-47* (New Delhi, pp. 223-245.
36. Kamaruddin, *East Pakistan*, p. 90.
37. Azad, I. W. F., p. 192.

Mountbatten reached Delhi on March 22 and was sworn in as Viceroy of India on 24th of the month. Immediately in his short speech, he stressed the need for a solution within the next few months.[38] Before assuming the office, the new Vcieroy had a discussion with Krishna Menon on March 13 when the latter advised him that there was no solution of Indian problem except the creation of Pakistan in the north-west and north-east areas of Indian sub-continent.[39] Mountbatten believed that the partition of India was the only solution from the present impasse, soon found ready acceptance to the idea in Patel's mind. Patel openly said that he was prepared to have a part of India if only he could get rid of the Muslim League. And when Patel was convinced, Mountbatten turned his attention to Nehru. Lord Mountbatten persisted till Jawaharlal's opposition was worn down step by step. Azad remarked "within a month of Lord Mountbatten's arrival in India, Jawaharlal, the firm opponent of partition had become, if not a supporter, at least acquiescent to the idea."[40]

The Viceroy's task became much easier by a "reorientation of the Congress attitude" for partition. In March, 1947, the choice of the Congress seemed to be between anarchy and partition and the Congress submitted themselves before the latter. The course of Indian history had already taken an inevitable turn before Mountbatten arrived in India. There was no room left for leaders to make or unmake history.

---

38. Mountbatten believed that he might have averted the partition of India, if he was to replace Wavell earlier in August, 1945.
39. Bandopadhyay. *Jinnha*, p 272.
40. Azad, I. W. F., p. 198.

CONCLUSION

Jawaharlal Nehru emerged as the de facto leader of the Congress after the failure of the Quit India movement. Gandhiji's theory of non-violence was not a soft-doctrine. It required supreme courage for the whole nation. Indian National Congress accepted non-violence, but not as a creed for all times and in all intentions. It was a very difficult times for Gandhiji, at least after the World War II. Gandhiji had no definite plan to lead India to independence. In 1945, he had no intention of offering civil disobedience movement or *Satyagrah.* History can never be repeated. The country now cannot go to 1942. Moreover Congress accepted non-violence when compelled by circumstances. Thus after the war Gandhiji was practically set aside, undertaking the cherished ideals of his life, the unity between the two major communities in India-Hindus and Muslims.

After the end of the war, the I. N. A. of Netaji Subhas emerged as the most popular among the masses more than the Congress. The Congress leaders, particularly of Nehru, were not the supporters of the I. N. A. for their joining hands with the Aix power. But the activities of the I. N. A. not only created a political spirit for freedom among the Indians, the British became convinced that they could no longer rely on the armed forces unless the political problem of India was solved.[1] The Congress bent down accordingly to gain political sympathy among the masses and soon it passed away as a temporary phase. The Congress accepted the policy of co-operation with the British for gaining Indian freedom.

After the formation of the Labour Government in England, the announcement of Attlee and sending of the Cabinet Mission accordingly, was the only positive document for India's freedom. Nehru offered his co-operation with the Cabinet Mission and Gandhiji at first believed that it was the best document the British Government could have produced. The acceptance of the Cabinet

1. Azad, I. W. F., p. 142.

Mission Plan by the Congress and the Leaque was a glorious event in Indian history though the latter accepted it by compelled circumstances. Jinnah thought that there could be no better than the plan. Jinnah initially admitted "that there could be no fairer solution of the minority problem than that presented in the Cabinet Mission Plan". But during his negotiations and discussions with the Cabinet Mission, the Muslim leader was not very happy. Meanwhile the statement of Nehru on July 10 showed a new way to Jinnah, who followed the policy of bloodshed and direct action against the Hindus. Nehru's statement on July 10, that the Congress could modify the Cabinet Mission Plan, raged the Muslim leader and gave opportunity for reviewing the whole situation. The statement of Nehru changed the view of Jinnah and the direct action of the Muslims was the greatest tragedy of Indian history for which Azad led the whole blame on Nehru. But this view of Azad could not be regarded as the true judgement of the situation. Jinnah after accepting the Cabinet Mission Plan, understood that he had been entraped which kept him aloof from the Muslim support on which he solely depended. The Muslims began to criticise him for closing down his tone in favour of Pakistan and joining hands with the Cabinet Mission, who had no scheme for Pakistan. Why then Jinnah led the Muslims fruitlessly for years on the dream of Pakistan ? During this time, Nehru's statement came to his rescue and he immediately resorted to direct action, combining once again almost all Muslims under his banner.

The Cabinet Mission, on the very outset, rejected the idea of Pakistan on the lines claimed by the Muslim League. They did not believe that the creation of Pakistan would solve the communal problem. True to their intention, the Mission soon involved in the impossible task of maintaining unity of India. Nehru had some ideals before him and so he was placed in the most disadvantageous position, pulled in two different directions by its left[2] and right wings, while Jinnah was the sole exponent

2. Jaya Prakash Narayan expressed his deep shock at the attitude of the Muslim League and accused it for stabbing at the back. He accused the Congress leaders as well, charging them for their compromising policy.

of the League. Thus Nehru could not act decisively and swifty. Gandhiji was too old and virtually renounced the leadership, Nehru was too ideals, while the Muslims looked to Patel with great enimity.

Jinnah's claim of forming the Interim Government, when rejected by the Viccroy, the former became out of temper. His prospect of capturing central government had vanished. He was then no longer interested to join in the constitution making body. The proposed Constituent Assembly seemed to him a trap that might destroy the very idea of Pakistan. On the question of parity with the League and the non-inclusion of a nationalist Muslim, Congress made constant opposition with the Cabinet Mission as well as with the League. Under such circumstance, the Muslim League withdrew on July 29, from the Cabinet Mission Plan and resorted to direct action.

The British government became greatly disgusted for the direct action of Jinnah. They realised a good shaking the League was 'badly needed' for Jinnah's outbrust. So Wavell, under the direction from London, invited Nehru to form the Interim Government. Jinnah believed in threats of force. After the Great Calcutta—Killing that disturbed the Provinces of Bengal and Bihar, communal violence became the strongest argument that gulded Jinnah for creating Pakistan. His "real freedom" could not be achieved without the division of Indian sub-continent. He made the meaning of freedom clear in his statement after the Great Calcutta-Killing : "We are not opposed to the freedom of the peoples of India, and we have made it clear that the only solution of India's problem is a division of India into Pakistan and Hindustan, which would mean real freedom for the two major nations."[3]

After the direct action and the formation of the Interim Government by the Congress, Wavell was bent upon bringing the League in the Coalition Government. He became fearful for Muslim League's direct action and realised a great disaster until

3. Jinnah's Statement, August 27, 1946 (S. I. N. C., II, p. ccxl).

a Congress-League coalition government was formed at the centre, and if possible, in the provinces. Inspite of the opposition of the Congress, Wavell became successful in bringing the League in the Coalition government. The League entred the government for conflict rather than co-operation with the Congress, while Nehru tried to establish Indian Republic through constitutional process. Soon after, the atmosphere in the Interim Government became so tense that the Congress members had twice threatened to resign. Thus Nehru charged the Viceroy for his failure to carry on the Interim Government in its original spirit. He also realised that the Viceroy and the League was gradually coming closer to each other.

In December 1946, two major parties, the Congress and the League, were called to London by the British Prime Minister to settle their differences amicably. The reluctant Nehru was also caught in the trap and the history began to change. From the proceedings of the London Conference, it became clear that Jinnah got sufficient encouragement to carry on his plan for non-accepting the Cabinet Mission Plan in its original principles though London conference itself was a departure from its original plan. The conference also set aside the formation of the Constituent Assembly for the whole of India by declaring that a Constituent Assembly framed by a majority should not be imposed upon the unwilling parts of the country. Thus the Cabinet Mission's delaration for an undivided India in the months of May-June 1946, became a distant cry in December 1946. The London Conference allowed the seeds of Pakistan to grow. Pakistan was allowed to nulify the verdict of the Federal Court.

In the London Conference, Nehru got vehement opposition from Cripps and Pethick Lawrence, once his supporters and also from Attlee, the British Prime Minister. On the other hand, Jinnah was encouraged by their support and more from the conservative party of Britain. Churchill vehemently criticised Nehru in British Parliament and held the latter responsible for communal outbrust in India. He even visualised a civil war against Congress attitude of establishing a Hindu majority rule in India. In case of dispute between the two communities, the British leaders even denied the necessity of referring the matter to the Federal Court. The Congress claimed that it was a departure from the principle of Cabinet Mission's original plan, fell into a deaf ear.[4] The Congress' complaint that it was the Muslim League who changed its decision, rejected the Cabinet Mission's scheme and resorted to direct action, also met the same result. The Muslim League's demand for the partition of India, which was also a nagation of Cabinet Mission's scheme, continued to get support from the British government after the London Conference.

The formation of independent Pakistan was the creation of Jinnah. For this purpose, he introduced the slogan of Two Nation theory. According to him, the Hindus and Muslims were two different races and culture, who could not live together. The seeds of Two Nation theory that Jinnah sowed in March 1940, grew with all its branches at the end of December 1946. It was Mohammad Iqbal, the poet, who instigated Jinnah for a separate state for the Muslims and wrote thirteen letters to him from May 1936 to November 1937. Jinnah gradually accepted the reason of his arguments. As early as in April 1940, Lord Lintithgow and Rajagopalachari accepted the theory of Pakistan. The Congress leaders, on the other hand tried to resist the partition up to the end of 1946, aiming at the independence of India as a whole.

The momentous declaration of Attlee on February 20, 1947, that the British would transfer power to responsible Indians within June 1948, hastened the Congress to decide the future of India. Nehru now began to proceed with an accelerated speed. The Congress cared little for various implications in the announcement. Gandhiji was then at Noakhali advocating for communal harmony. He was not prepared to go to Delhi and participate in the political tangle. He advised the Congress, not to accept any arrangement in a hurry, which they might have to repent at leisure. He

4. The Congress pointed out in their statement on December 22, 1946, that the Viceroy accepted the principle of referring dispute to the Federal Court on June 28 and again on August 24.

warned the Congress to be prepared for worse, instead of India's partition. But the Congress leaders, judged the situation in terms of political necessity, fearing that delay might drift the country to a civil war.

Congress accepted partition before the arrival of Mountfatten. Nehru, Patel, Kripalani, Krishna Menon, all of them accepted the partition of India as a lesser evil. But the partition could not solve the communal problem in the country. India gained her freedom but lost her unity. The creation of Pakistan weakened the position of the Muslims in Indian sub-continent.

The Muslim League had never taken any part in the political struggle and as such had a few leaders of national importance. After the end of the war, it was no longer the British Raj but the League that stood in the way of national movement. So the British secretly supported the League. League's success in harrassing the Congress from October 1946 to March 1947 was due to the policies of Wavell. Pakistan was created on the basis of Jinnah's Two Nation theory but ultimately that theory also became a failure, as the creation of Bangladesh would testify.

Gandhiji's theory of non-violence was also fell into disuse by his followers. They followed the policy of negotiations with the British for India's freedom. Negotiations could not create strong determination among them. Naturally the British were in an advantageous position than the Congress, who could dictate to the latter whatever they pleased. As a result the dawn of freedom appeared through India's partitian.

Nehru was a great patriot, who made immense contributions for India's freedom. He was an idealist but that sometime stood on the way of India's unity. At the same time, he was vain and sometimes was not ready to listen the views of others that clashed with him Sometimes, he and his followers could not take prompt decision, as in the case of joining in the Interim-Government. While after Attlee's announcement on February 20, he and the other Congress leaders accepted the unusual hasty decision for India's freedom. The admixture of vacillation and hasty decisions among the Congress leaders, gave Jinnah the opportunity to divide India.

The diastrous second world war was the decisive factor for achieving India's freedom. America who rescued Britain from the war, pressurised her for India's co-operation in future to arrest the progress of communism. England, on the other hand, had been torn by the war, whose racial and naval superiority had been challenged. The Labour Government faced economic crisis within, which neeeded urgent improvement. Meanwhile the Allies witnessed British imperialism as well as her incompetency to face Germany and Japan. It was feared that India might go to communism, which was spreading rapidly after the second world war. Under such critical situation, co-operation with India was very essential. So Indian independence was a necessity for Britain, sooner or later, which, our Indian leaders could not realise. As a result, the dawn of our freedom came through partition.

BIBLIOGRAPHY

1. Primary Sources

—*A Bunch of old letters* by Jawaharlal Nehru, New York, 1960.

—All India Congress Committee papers.

—Indian Annual Registrar, vol. 11, 1946.

—Important Speeches of Jawaharlal Nehru, vols 1 and 2 Edt. by J. S. Bright.

—J. N. Papers (NMML).

—Jawaharlal Nehru's Speeches, 1946-64, 5 vols. Government of India Publication 1949-69.

—Nehru, the first sixty years, vol. II, Selected and edited by Dorothy Norman, Bombay, 1965.

—Nehru's letter to his Sister, by Krishna Nehru Huthesing, London, 1963.

—Speeches and documents on Indian Constitution, 1921-47 by Gwyer Maurice and A. Appadorai, London, 1957.

—Selected Writings on Jawaharlal Nehru, 1916-50, Edt. by J. S. Bright, New Delhi, 1950.

—Selected works of Jawaharlal Nehru, vol. I, General Editor, S. Gopal, New Delhi, 1972.

—Vijayalaxmi Pandit Papers (NMML).

2. Secondary Sources

(A) *English*

—Alexander, H. G., *India since Cripps*, London, 1944.

—Ahmad, Kamaruddin, *The Social history of East Pakistan*, Dacca, 2nd Edn., 1957.

—Azad, Abul Kalam, *India wins freedom*, New Delhi, Reprint, 1989.

—Agarwala, R. N., *National Movement and Constitutional development of India*, Delhi, 1956.

—Aziz, K. K., *Britain and Muslim India*, London, 1963.

—Bright, J. S., *Before and after Independence*, New Delhi, 1950.

—Bright, J. S., *The life of Jawaharlal Nehru*, New Delhi, 1958.

—Bolitho, Hector, *Jinnah*, London, 1960.

—Birla, G. D., *In the Shadow of Mahatma*, Orient Longman 1953.

—Bose, Nirmal Kumar, *Studies in Gandhism*, Caloutto, 1947.

—Brecher, Minchael, *Nehru : A political biography*, London, 1959.

—Brown, Judith, *Gandhi's Rise to Power*, Combridge, 1972.

—Campbell-Johnson, Alan, *Mission with Mountbatten*, London, 1951.

—Cousins, N., *Talks with Nehru*, London, 1951.

—Dhawan, G. N., *The political philosophy of Mahatma Gandhi*, Ahmedabad, 1951.

—Douglas, I. H., *Abul Kalam Azad : An Intellectual and Religious Biography*, Delhi, 1988.

—Dutt, R. Palm, *India Today*, Bombay, 1947.

—Fischer, Louis, *The life of Mahatma Gandhi*, New York, 1962.

—Ghosh, K. K., *The Indian National Army*,

—Hardy P., *The Muslims of British India*, London, 1972.

—Hodson, H. V., *The Greet Divide : Britain-India-Pakistan*, London, 1969.

—Jalal, Ayesha, *The Sole Spokesman : Jinnah, the Muslim League and the Demand of Pakistan, Cambridge*, 1985.

—Kabir, Humayun, *Muslim Politics, 1906-47*, Delhi, 1969.

—Kripalani, J. B., *Gandhi : His life and thought*, New Delhi, 1970.

—Law, D. A. (Edt), *The Indian National Congress : Centenary Hindsights*, Delhl, 1988.

—Lapping, Brian, *The Last days of Raj*, London, 1975.

—Lohiya, Rammanohar, *Guilty men of India's partition*, Hyderabad, 1970.

—Lumby, E. W. R., *The Transfer of Power in India*, London, 1954.

—Macmillan, Harold, *Tides of Fortune, 1945-55*, London, 1969.

—Manserg, N., *The Transfer of Power*, vol. II, London, 1958.

—Mazumdar, R. C, *History of the Freedom Movement in India*, vol. III, Calcutta, 1963.

—Majumdar, S. K., *Jinnah and Gandhi–their roles in India's Quest for freedom*, Calcutta, 1966.

—Moon, Panderel, *Gandhi and Modern India*, London, 1968.

—Moon, Panderel, *Divide and Quit*, London, 1962.

—Moore, R. J., *Escape from Empire : The Attlee Government and the Indian Problem*, New York, 1983.

—Menon, V. P., *The Transfer of Power in India*, New Jersey, 1957.

—Muller Edward and Bhattacharjee, Arun, *India wins Independence*, New Delhi, 1988.

—Moraes, Frank, *Jawaharlal Nehru*, New York, 1956.

—Mosley, Leonard, *The last days of the British Raj*, London, 1961.

—Munshi, K. M., *Pilgrimage to freedom*, Bombay, 1967.

—Narasimhaiah, C. D., *Jawaharlal Nehru*, Mysore, 1959.

—Nanda, B. R, *Mahatma Gandhi–a Biography*, London, 1958.

—Nanda, B. R., *The Nehrus*, London, 1965.

—Naim, C. M. (Edt), *Iqbal, Jinnah and Pakistan*, Delhi, 1982.

—Nehru, Jawaharlal, *Discovery of India*, Indian Reprint, 1967.

——————, *An Autobiography*, Indian Edn., 1962.

——————, *Independence and After 1946-49*, Delhi, 1949,

—Pandey, B. N., *Nehru*, London, Reprint, 1977.

—Pal, J. J., *Jinnah and the Creation of Pakistan*, Delhi, 1983.

—Parikh, N. D., *Sardar Vallabhbhai Patel*, vols, I, II, Ahmedabad 1953, 1956.

—Prasad, Rajendra, *Autobiography*, Muzaffarpur, 1947.

—Philips, C. H., *The Evolution of India and Pakistan*, London, 1962.

—Pyarelal, *Mahatma Gandhi-the last Phase*, vol. I, Ahmedabad, 1956.

—Ram Gopal, *Indian Muslims—A Political history*, Bombay, 1959.

—Saied, M. H., *The Sound of Fury—A political study of Mohammad Ali Jinnah*, New Delhi, 1981.

—Sen, Shila, *Muslim politics in Bengal*, 1937-47, New Delhi, 1976.

—Seton, Marie, *Panditiji : A portrait of Jawaharlel Nehru*, London, 1967.

—Singh, Anita Inder, *The Origins of the Partition of India, 1936-47*, Delhi, 1987.

—Sitaramayya, Pattabhi, *History of Indian National Congress*, Vol. II, New Delhi, 1969.

—Spear, Percival, *India, Pakistan and the West*, London, 1958.

—Symonds, Richard, *The Making of Pakistan*, London, 1950.

—Talukdar, M. H. R. (Edt.), *Memories of H. S. Suhrawardy*, Dacca, 1987.

—Tendulkar, D. G., *Mahetma : Life of Mohandas Karamchand Gandhi*, 8 vols., Bombay, 1951-54.

—Tinker, Hugh, *Experlment with Froedom : India and Pakistan*, London, 1967.

—Toye, Hugh, *The Springing Tiger*, Bombay, 1959.

—Woolpert, Stenley, *Jinnah of Pakistan*, New York, 1984.

—Zakaria, Rafiq (Edt.), *A Study of Nehru*, Bombay, 1959.

(B) Bengali

—Bandopadhyay, Sailesh Kumar, *Jinnah : Pakistan, Natun Bhabna*, 2nd Edn., Calcutta, 1396 B. S.

—Chaudhuri, Binayendra Mohan, *Bivakta Bharat*, Visva Bharati, 1356 B. S.

—Dasgupta, Surajit, *Islam O Bharat*, Calcutta.

—De, Sailesh, *Aami Subhas Bolchi*, Calcutta, 3rd Ed., 1989 B. S.

—Tripathi, Amalesh, *Bharater Swadhinata Sangrame Jatiya Congress*, Calcutta, 1989.

(C) Journals and Newspapers

—Ananda Bazar Patrika, Calcutta.

—Amrita Bazar Patrika, Calcutta.

—Hindustan Times, Delhi.

—The Searchlight, Patna.

—The Hindu, Madras.

—Times of India, Delhi.

—Visva-Bharati Quarterly, Santiniketan.

—Voice of India, Washington.

—Wavell, Lord, The Viceroy's Journal, Edt. by Penderal Moon, London, 1973.

INDEX